THE HOLY SPIRIT AND HIS GIFTS

Contemporary Evangelical Perspectives Series

THE HOLY SPIRIT AND HIS GIFTS

J. Oswald Sanders

Consulting Director, Overseas Missionary Fellowship

Lamplighter Books
Grand Rapids, Michigan
Zondervan Publishing House

Lamplighter Books are published by Zondervan
Publishing House, 1415 Lake Drive, S.E.,
Grand Rapids, Michigan 49506

THE HOLY SPIRIT AND HIS GIFTS
Formerly issued as *The Holy Spirit of Promise*

Library of Congress Catalog Card Number: 76-120032

Printed in the United States of America

86   87   88   89 / 24   23   22

CONTENTS

INTRODUCTION

As this book has been in circulation for thirty years, the need for a revision is obvious. During the intervening years there has been a considerable increase in interest in the doctrine of the Holy Spirit, and an increased hunger on the part of many for a deeper experience of His working in their hearts and service. This gives great cause for thanksgiving.

Few biblical doctrines have caused such division and acrimony within the Church as this. One of the most subtle tactics adopted by the Enemy to paralyse the Church, has been to make Christians afraid of the Holy Spirit. He has driven groups of earnest believers to adopt extreme positions on the right and on the left. He laughs as he sees neither group in complete enjoyment of the power and fulness the Spirit delights to bestow. It is stark tragedy that the doctrine which is intended to produce "the unity of the Spirit", becomes a fruitful source of disunity. Carnal opposition to extremes of teaching on this subject has just as baneful effects on church and individual as the teaching itself. It was in this very connection that Paul advocated the excellence of love.

It has been my endeavour to present the correct doctrine of the Holy Spirit, as I understand it, yet in untheological language; to win for the Holy Spirit a deeper recognition and love from those in whom He deigns to dwell; to constantly relate the doctrinal aspects of this subject to the practical life and experience of the Christian; to endeavour to answer in an uncontentious manner some of the controversial aspects of the doctrine current today, especially in relation to the baptism and the gifts of the Spirit.

In order that readers may have the benefit of the views of acknowledged authorities on this subject, each chapter is preceded by two or three quotations selected from the writings of a score of evangelical scholars. The pages are liberally sprinkled with Scripture references for the use of those who desire to verify for themselves the validity of the views expressed.

Many books have been consulted in the preparation of this

volume, and a list of the chief of these will be found in the bibliography at the end. Unfortunately this revision has been made away from my library, and I am unable to append the publishers and dates.

J. OSWALD SANDERS

Auckland
New Zealand

Chapter One

THE DISPLACED MEMBER
OF THE GODHEAD

"One of the greatest failures in Christian thought and practice has to do with the Holy Spirit. Far too often Christians have assumed that the Spirit and His operation are easier to understand than, say, the person and work of Christ. In almost every age too little attention has been paid to pneumatology (the doctrine of the Holy Spirit), and this has resulted in a distortion of Christian doctrine and an impoverishment of Christian life and work."

GEOFFREY W. BROMILEY

" 'No, we have never heard that there is a Holy Spirit.' Such was the reply of the Ephesian disciples to St. Paul's question 'Did you receive the Holy Spirit when you believed!' Their word express a state of mind to which the modern Church, to put it mildly, is no stranger. The Holy Spirit has justly been described as 'the displaced person of the Godhead.' The presence in some quarters of strange and distorted views about the Spirit's operations is regrettable, but much more regrettable is the widespread absence of true teaching."

A. M. STIBBS

"And how can now the Spirit thus be known? Jesus says: 'Ye know Him, for He abideth with you and shall be in you.' The abiding indwelling of the Spirit is the condition of knowing Him. His presence will be self-evidencing. As we allow Him to dwell in us, as we give Him full possession in faith and obedience, and allow Him to testify of Jesus as Lord, He will bring His credentials: He will prove Himself to be the Spirit of God. 'It is the Spirit beareth witness, because the Spirit is truth.' It is because the presence of the Spirit as the indwelling Teacher of every believer is so little known and recognised in the Church, and because, as the result of this, the workings of the Spirit are few and feeble, that there is so much difficulty, and doubt, so much fear and hesitation about the recognition of the witness of the Spirit. As the truth and experience of the indwelling of the Spirit is restored among God's people, and the Spirit is free again to work in power among us, His blessed presence will be its own sufficient proof: we shall indeed know Him."

ANDREW MURRAY

THE DISPLACED MEMBER
OF THE GODHEAD

*"Did you receive the Holy Spirit when you believed?
And they said unto Him, 'No, we have not even heard
whether there be a Holy Spirit'."*

Acts 19:2 NASB

*"The Spirit of truth Whom the world cannot receive,
because it does not behold Him or know Him, but* you
know Him, *because He abides with you and will be in
you."*

John 14:17 NASB

"In most Christian churches the Spirit is entirely overlooked.
Whether He is present or absent makes no real difference to anyone. Brief reference is made to Him in the Doxology and the
Benediction. Further than that, He might as well not exist. So
completely do we ignore Him that it is only by courtesy that we
can be called Trinitarian. . . . The idea of the Spirit held by the
average church member is so vague as to be nearly non-existent."
These trenchant words from the pungent pen of A. W. Tozer,
even if only partially true, should challenge us to remedy this
grave deficiency which is paralysing the effectiveness of our
churches.

Jesus said of His disciples in the Upper Room *"But ye know
Him*—the Spirit of truth." This was doubtless true of them,
but is it equally true of all His disciples today? Do we really
know Him? Judging by the place accorded to Him in contemporary hymnology, theology and preaching, the general level of
knowledge of the Spirit is scant indeed. It is possible to sit
through a year's sermons without hearing one which specifically
honours the Third Person of the Trinity. He has become the displaced member of the Godhead, and the Church has endeavoured to compensate for His absence by substituting elaborate
machinery and programmes for the dynamic of the Spirit. Small
wonder that the witness of the Church in a world *in extremis*
has grown anaemic and her influence minimal.

10

Ye know Him

A preacher was about to deliver a carefully prepared message when there came to him the conviction that it was not appropriate to the group of people before him. He reluctantly abandoned his manuscript, and seeking the Spirit's guidance, decided to read John chapter fourteen.

As he read, he was alert to discern the message for the occasion. Nor was he disappointed. On reaching verse seven, three words gripped his attention—"Ye know Him"—God the Father. He read two more verses, and a second clause became luminous, "Hast thou not known me?"—God the Son. When he reached verse seventeen, a third sentence arrested him, "But ye know Him"—God the Holy Spirit.

These words struck home with tremendous force. Did he really know Him? "I know God the Father," he mused, "and have experienced much of His paternal love and care. I know God the Son, for is He not my Saviour with whom I daily commune? But I cannot say that I know the Holy Spirit in any comparable and personal way."

This experience of the author led to a more comprehensive study of the Scriptures relating to the ministry of the Holy Spirit, and resulted in the personal knowledge of Him which had previously been lacking.

Knowledge by Experience

In answer to Paul's enquiry, "Did you receive the Holy Spirit when you believed?" the twelve disciples of John replied, "No, we have not even heard whether there be a Holy Spirit." Not many church members would return such an answer today, for they are familiar with the creed: "I believe in the Holy Ghost." Yet to some the Spirit is still "it" rather than "He". They know there is a Holy Spirit, but conceive of Him as an ethereal influence or intangible power—but not as a real divine Person who can be known and loved and worshipped.

Some are orthodox in doctrine and know a great deal *about* the Spirit, but do not *know* Him in the sense implied in this clause. This distinction is not an arbitrary one, but is extremely important, for the word "know" here means knowledge which is the outcome of experience, not mere intellectual apprehension. It is one thing to know about a celebrity, but quite another to know him personally.

The difference is like that between knowing all about food, even possessing it, and eating and enjoying it. One is intellectual apprehension, the other is knowledge gained by experience. It is not knowing *about* God that brings eternal life, but knowing God,[1] surely a vital distinction. But there is no reason why searching to know about the Spirit should not lead to our getting to know Him by personal acquaintance.

Once the crucially important role the Holy Spirit fills in the life and experience of the Christian is grasped, to ignore His gracious presence or neglect His inner working will be seen to be inexcusable and foolish.

Intangible and Impersonal

Reasons and excuses for such ignorance and neglect, inadequate though they be, are not difficult to discover. In thinking of the Spirit, we are apt to confuse personality with corporeality. Because He assumed no bodily form we tend to conceive of the Spirit as an intangible, impersonal force or influence emanating from God—"a nebulous something like a wisp of invisible smoke which is said to be in churches, and to hover over good people when they are dying."

But personality is altogether independent of the body. It is spiritual, not physical. When all that is mortal lies in dust, the personality still exists. The Christian who has died is without a body until the resurrection, but his essential personality is in no way affected by death. Beyond the grave he still feels and thinks and wills.[2] While it is true that the Holy Spirit cannot be seen or heard speaking in an audible voice, we can nevertheless know and feel His personal presence and hear His voice as "Spirit to spirit He doth speak."

Contrasted with the other Persons of the Godhead, the Holy Spirit does indeed seem impersonal. The visible creation renders the person of the *Father* easy of conception. He presents a familiar figure, a concrete frame of reference. The incarnation and historical life of the *Son*, the Man of Nazareth, makes disbelief in His personality well nigh impossible. But the operations of the *Spirit* are so mysterious that we are prone to discount the reality of His personality. There seems to be no definite and familiar thought pattern into which we can fit Him. Compared with the Father and the Son, He seems elusive and impersonal.

Colour is lent to this idea by the names accorded to Him in Scripture—Holy Spirit, Holy Ghost—which tend to convey the impression of an impersonal influence rather than a divine

Person. The symbols and emblems used to interpret His nature and operations—fire, wind, oil—also conduce to the same end. The fact that in Greek "Spirit" is neuter appears to lend support to this misconception. But in point of fact, the Holy Spirit is represented by the neuter forms of "parakleton" and "pneuma";[3] by the masculine pronoun "ekeinos";[4] while by the function of birth,[5] the feminine is suggested. Hence, as all the genders cannot be predicated of any one personality, it would be correct to infer that when applied to the Holy Spirit, the pronoun "it" is used in a sexless way.

Personality in the Godhead

In referring to the Holy Spirit as a Person, our statements and conceptions need safeguarding, for the term cannot be carried over from the human to the Divine without qualification. As applied to the Godhead, the term "person" does not mean exactly the same as when applied to man. The inadequacy of human language to express divine truth makes it necessary to use words which most nearly convey the desired thought.

In His efforts to unfold the mysteries of His own nature and being, God makes use of illustrations drawn from the moral nature of man whom He made in His own image and likeness, so that by means of these terms of accommodation, we may think our way up to Him. Without the use of such anthropomorphic terms and illustrations, we could not conceive of God at all. Inadequate though the word "person" may be, no other term has been found which so fully expresses the essential distinctions within the Godhead.

As applied to man, the term "person" implies the existence of a separate, self-conscious human being, distinct from all others. When used of the Godhead, however, it carries no such significance. There is no idea of three separate Beings. The Father, the Son, and the Spirit are three Persons, but not three separate, distinct Beings. Each is distinct from the other, but none is separate from the other in the substratum of existence.

An inadequate illustration,—and all illustrations bearing on the Godhead are inadequate—may shed at least one ray of light on what is admittedly a most baffling problem. In my home I may be variously related to three women. To one I stand in the relation of husband, to another I am father, to a third, employer. I am only one man, but in my home I bear a threefold relation. All three recognize me in each of those relations, but I am related to each only in the relationship peculiar to them.

13

The term "person", then, as applied to members of the Godhead, is intended to express the idea of an inner distinction which exists within the unity of the Divine Nature. The Holy Spirit is distinct from the Father and the Son, yet shares the same inseparable life.

Personality of the Holy Spirit

The essential elements of personality—intelligence, emotion, volition and action—are all ascribed in Scripture to the Holy Spirit. We read of "the *mind* of the Spirit",[6] "the *love* of the Spirit",[7] "the *will* of the Spirit",[8] and of the activities of the Spirit.[9] He possesses in infinite degree those qualities in man which persist beyond the grave.

The Spirit speaks of Himself and is spoken of in distinctly personal terms. "The Holy Spirit said, 'Separate me Barnabas and Saul for the work whereunto I have called them'."[10] Paul and Silas were "forbidden of the Holy Spirit to preach the Word in Asia."[11] His more prominent official title, "Paraclete"[12] is the same term as is used of Christ.[13] Such a designation would not be appropriate to an abstract influence but only to a person.

Chrysostom wrote, "By the word 'another', Christ shows the distinction of persons; by the word 'Paraclete' He declares the equality of dignity." In His discourse in the Upper Room, our Lord repeatedly used personal pronouns in speaking of the Spirit. "I will send *Him* unto you."[14] "*He* will teach you all things."[15] Sound exegesis demands that in such passages the Holy Spirit be regarded as a Person.

He is personal in His relations with men. He dwells in men as a personal inhabitant in the believer whose body is His temple.[16] From the fact that He can be grieved, personality must be predicated. Can an influence be grieved? The word necessarily implies the power to love, for only love can be grieved. One cannot "blaspheme" an influence, or "speak against" an abstract power. And yet it is possible to blaspheme the Holy Spirit.[17] In this very passage blaspheming the Spirit is said to be followed by infinitely more serious consequences than blaspheming the Son of Man. Would it not be anomalous if blaspheming the power or influence of God was a greater crime than blaspheming God Himself?

The activities of which the Spirit is author and the functions He fulfils add to the increasing weight of evidence in favour of His personality. He is the Teacher and Guide, apart from whose illumination man cannot apprehend divine truth,[18] a function for which personality is obviously essential. The work of creation

14

is attributed to him.[19] As though to safeguard the truth of His own personality, the Holy Spirit is careful to distinguish His gifts from Himself. "There are diversities of gifts but the same Spirit."[20]

Some with Unitarian leanings have endeavoured to dismiss the ascription to the Spirit of personal subsistence distinct from the Father and the Son as mere personification. A simple but sufficient answer to this contention would be to invite its proponent to substitute "power" for "Holy Spirit" in the following passages, and note the redundancy. "God anointed Jesus of Nazareth with power and with power."[21] "That ye may abound in hope through the power of the power."[22] "In demonstration of the power and of power."[23]

Viewing the testimony of Scripture as a whole, we cannot but concede consistent, and clear testimony to the fact that the Holy Spirit is a Divine Person, working with intelligent consciousness, infinite love and independent will. This fact and truth is of fundamental importance to Christian experience. If He is merely a power or influence, our dominant aim would be, "How may I obtain more of His power and influence?" But if He is a Divine Person, our consistent attitude should be "How can He more fully possess me so that I may become the vehicle of His power and influence?"

REFERENCES

1. John 17:3.   2. Luke 16:23–31.   3. John 14:16.   4. John 16:13, 14.
5. John 3:5.   6. Rom. 8:27.   7. Rom. 15:30.   8. 1 Cor. 12:11.
9. 1 Cor. 12:11.   10. Acts 13:2.   11. Acts 16:6, 7.   12. John 15:26.
13. 1 John 2:1.   14. John 16:7.   15. John 14:26.   16. 1 Cor.
16:9.   17. Matt. 12:31-2.   18. John 14:26.   19. Psa. 104:30.
20. 1 Cor. 12:4.   21. Acts 10:38.   22. Rom. 15:13.   23. 1 Cor. 2:4.

Chapter Two

THE PROMISED COMFORTER

" 'It is expedient for you,' says Jesus, 'that I go away.' If it was expedient for them that He should go away in order that the Comforter might come, does this not imply that the Spirit's advent would compensate, ay, and more than compensate the Church for any loss she might sustain from the want of the Saviour's bodily presence? We sometimes hear men say that if they had lived in the Saviour's day, if they had been permitted to hear His voice and to witness His miracles, it would be better for them than it is. And yet the very lesson that Jesus here teaches is that their future condition would not be worse but better when He should leave them, because the Holy Spirit would descend."

CHARLES ROSS

"The Holy Spirit during the present time is in office on earth; and all spiritual presence and divine communion of the Trinity with men are through Him. In other words, while the Father and the Son are visibly and personally in heaven, they are invisibly here in the body of the faithful by the indwelling of the Comforter. So that though we affirm that on the Day of Pentecost the Holy Spirit came to dwell upon earth for this entire dispensation, we do not imply that He thereby ceased to be in heaven. Not with God, as with finite man, does arrival in one place necessitate withdrawal from another. Jesus uttered a saying concerning Himself so mysterious and seemingly contradictory that many attempts have been made to explain away its literal and obvious meaning : 'And no man hath ascended up to heaven but He that came down from heaven, even the Son of man Who is in heaven'—Christ on earth, and yet in glory; here and there, at the same time, just as a thought which we embody in speech and send forth from the mind, yet remains in the mind as really and distinctly as before it was expressed."

A. J. GORDON

"When Christ ascended in bodily form to the Father, at Pentecost He sent in spiritual form the Holy Spirit, to be His 'Other Comforter'. So that the Holy Spirit continues and develops spiritually what Christ in His flesh initiated in the days of His humanity. The Holy Spirit continually and permanently applying Christ's finished work historically from Calvary, contemporarily to every new generation of people living in this world."

M. A. P. WOOD

THE PROMISED COMFORTER

"I will pray the Father and He shall give you another Comforter, that He may abide with you forever...."
John 14:16

"It is expedient for you that I go away.... If I depart, I will send Him unto you."
John 16:7

"I will not leave you orphans, I will come to you."
John 14:18 (*Alford*)

"Another Comforter! Another Paraclete!" When first these words fell on their ears, they afforded little comfort to the bewildered, apprehensive disciples of Jesus. Their Master had opened His heart to them, and the import of His words was beginning to stir dark forebodings. "One of you shall betray me." "Whither I go, thou canst not follow me now."[1] "I go to prepare a place for you." And now He is saying, "Yet a little while and the world seeth me no more."[2]

What do these mystifying statements mean? Surely they cannot imply that He is going to leave them! Gradually He breaks to them in plain, unmistakable words the shattering truth they had been so reluctant to believe. "Ye have heard how I said unto you, I go away, and come again to you. If ye loved me, ye would rejoice because I said, I go to the Father."[3]

Yes, He is going to leave them. But what then? How can they go on living when the light of their life has gone out? How face a menacing world without His supporting presence? How could any Comforter fill the place He had held in their lives? His assurance sounded hollow and insubstantial in their ears: "I tell you the truth, it is to your advantage that I go away."[4] Could anything be more to their advantage, more in their best interests than His continued presence with them? Small wonder they were overwhelmed. A mother's death in the best interests of her little children!

When they thought of His impending departure, the icy hand of despair clutched at their hearts. But when their feeble faith gripped His promise, unintelligible though it seemed, hope sprang afresh in their breasts. Had He not promised that He would not cast them off as orphans,[5] implying that in some inscrutable way He would fill the blank in their lives that His departure would create? He had done so many other impossible things; perhaps He could do even this. So they wavered between hope and despair.

An orphan has known a father, a mother, the sweetness of home, but has lost them. The disciples were soon to find themselves in just such a position, alone in a hostile world, lambs in the midst of wolves. But He assured them that His departure would not be like that of a father whose children were left orphans when he died. "In the Spirit, I am coming back to you," He assured them. Just as the orphaned child on the day of the parent's death needs someone to strengthen and comfort him, so Jesus promised to send the Holy Spirit, the Comforter, to support the Twelve through the darkness and desolation following His death.

Comforter or Strengthener?

"Comforter" is universally admitted to be an unfortunate and inadequate translation of the Greek "paraclete." Samuel Chadwick goes so far as to say that "the translation entirely misses the mark and is responsible for untold mischief in both doctrine and experience. . . . It misrepresents the mission of the Spirit, has led believers to think less of obligation than of comfort, and has associated religion with soothing consolations rather than with conflict. The need is not comfort, but power." While agreeing with the sentiments he expresses so forcefully, it would not be wrong to affirm that the title includes something of both meanings.

It was John Wycliffe who was responsible for the appearance of the word "Comforter" in our Bible. But today it carries a far different meaning from that which it bore in the fourteenth century. Then, as the Latin words from which it is derived indicate, its root significance was strength. Indeed this meaning was obviously in Wycliffe's mind, for he translated Paul's startling affirmation in his Philippian letter, "I can do all things through Christ who *comforts* me."[6] To him the word conveyed the idea of strengthener, helper.

Since then its significance has been greatly diluted, until today it is associated in our minds almost exclusively with consolation and comfort in sorrow and trouble. From its derivation we rightly deduce that it conveys the idea of strengthening, empowering in weakness. But from our Lord's words, "I will not leave you orphans," we also rightly infer that the thought of comfort in sorrow is not absent.

It is noteworthy, however, that in not one of the four instances in which the word was used by our Lord in the Upper Room discourse was the thought of sorrow prominent in His mind. In two instances the Comforter is identified as the Spirit of truth, who was to lead the disciples into all truth.[7] In the third instance, His function is said to be that of remembrancer of and witness to Christ.[8] In the last instance the Spirit is seen convicting the human heart "of sin, righteousness and judgment."[9] From our Lord's usage of the word, it becomes clear that, while present, the idea of consolation and comfort is distinctly secondary to that of strength and help.

Because the Revisers were far from satisfied that "Comforter" was the most felicitous translation of the word, they introduced the alternative words "Advocate or Helper" in the margin of the English Revised Version. The substitution of "Advocate" for "Comforter" in John 14-16 conveys much more accurately the sense of the word. But perhaps a still better method of procedure would be to naturalize and carry over into our vocabulary the Greek word "Paraclete," as has frequently been done with other words for which an accurate translation is difficult to attain.

The Divine Advocate

The Latin word "Advocate" is a close equivalent of the Greek "paraclete," and the figure throws much light on the work of the Holy Spirit. Both words share the meaning, "to call to one's side for help," especially against an accuser or judge. This has led to the Spirit being referred to as "the Divine Barrister". The ideal barrister of former days assumed a fourfold obligation when he undertook a case. He was his client's representative, pleaded his cause, defended his name and guarded and administered his property.

Such is the work of the Divine Advocate. But on whose behalf? It may come as a surprise to some to learn that the Holy Spirit is not our Advocate, but Christ's. Did Jesus not say He would send *"another* Paraclete," thus implying that He was one Paraclete and the Spirit was the other? John's statement gives confirmation of this: "If any man sin, we have an Advocate with the Father, Jesus Christ the righteous."[10] The Son is our Advocate with the Father in heaven, but the Spirit is the Advoate of the Son on earth. Like the ideal barrister, it is His office to represent Christ, plead His cause, defend His name and protect the interests of His Kingdom, an office which He zealously fulfils.

On the other hand we, as the disciples, can draw strength and comfort from our Lord's word, "*another* Comforter" for the word signifies "*another of the same kind*". The Holy Spirit is Jesus' other Self—He was given to be to us on earth all that our Lord would be were He personally present. He said, "*another* Paraclete," not a "*different*" Paraclete, one like Himself who would take His place and do His work. In the person of His Spirit, Christ has come and is constantly at our side to strengthen and help.

In His parting message, Jesus warned His disciples of the treatment they could expect at the hands of a hostile world. "If the world hate you," He said, "ye know that it hated me before it hated you . . . If they have persecuted me, they will also persecute you."[11] In this time of trial, He points them to the Advocate by whom they would be victorious over the opposition of the world.

The Expedient Departure

From our vantage-point, it is not difficult to grasp the expediency of our Lord's departure, with the resulting gift of the Holy Spirit, but to the disciples it must have been well-nigh incomprehensible. In what possible way could the spiritual presence of the Holy Spirit be preferred to the physical presence of the human Jesus? How could Christ's absence enrich rather than impoverish them? Jesus could have made this statement only if His going would mean not a tragic absence, but His presence on a higher plane, bringing with it a new and hitherto unknown intimacy. And this is exactly what His promise meant to convey.

In His earthly life, Jesus was geographically limited by His body. He could not be in two places at once. When He was in Nazareth, Jerusalem was denied His comforting presence. When He was having a private talk with Peter, James was deprived of the sunshine of His smile. At best His disciples' contact with Him could be only occasional, and His influence on them only from without. His presence with them in time of temptation had robbed it of its power to allure. But it was very much otherwise when He was absent from their side.

In contrast to this, when the heavenly Paraclete was given, they would exchange Christ's physical presence for His omnipresence.

Being Himself omnipresent, the Holy Spirit does not know the limitations of a human body, but is equally accessible to all God's people wherever they are and whatever their need. Moreover, His is an internal and not an external presence. From within the regenerated heart He carries on His sanctifying work, revealing Christ and reproducing His likeness.

Not until Jesus "breathed on them and said, 'Receive ye the Holy Spirit' "[12] did the apprehensive disciples realize the joyous significance of their Master's enigmatical statement, "It is expedient for you that I go away". No longer would they need His visible and bodily presence among them; they would have something better.

> *"What though His holy footsteps*
> *Linger no longer here?*
> *Still through His Spirit's presence*
> *Jesus is ever near,*
> *What though your heart be lonely*
> *What though your friends be few,*
> *He will not leave you orphans,*
> *Jesus will come to you."*

"He shall send you another Comforter that He may abide with you forever."[13] The Divine Paraclete has come to stay. He seals the believer's heart "unto the day of redemption".[14] He may be grieved, and through our sin we may lose the sense of His approval, but He will never leave the heart which He has transformed into His temple.

REFERENCES

1. John 13:21, 36. 2. John 14:1, 19. 3. John 14:28. 4. John 16:7 (Weymouth). 5. John 14:18. 6. Phil. 4:13. 7. John 14:16, 15:26. 8. John 14:26. 9. John 16:8. 10. 1 John 2:1. 11. John 15:18, 30. 12. John 20:22. 13. John 14:16. 14. Eph. 4:30.

Chapter Three

THE DEITY OF THE SPIRIT

"The deity of the Holy Spirit has been a cardinal doctrine of the Christian faith from the beginning. The Arian controversy in the fourth century of the Christian era settled for all time the orthodox doctrine on both the personality and the deity of the Spirit. Arius, who held that the Holy Spirit was a created being, though he adhered originally to the personality of the Spirit later denied both His personality and deity. His views were denounced by his contemporaries, and Arius was branded a heretic. From that day to this, orthodox Christianity has affirmed the deity and personality of the Spirit."

JOHN F. WALVOORD

"It were easy to prove the personality of David or St. John from the individual character of each, from the works they wrought, and the sufferings they endured. But these characteristics and actions and passions were those of men, not of God; human, not Divine; such as appertain to the creature, and not to the Creator. With regard to the Holy Ghost, however, such are the attributes which He is represented as possessing, such the operations which He performs, such the supreme dignity which Scripture, by comparing spiritual things with spiritual, ascribes to Him, and such the intimate relationship in which He stands to the Father and the Son, that One to whom these qualities are attributed, and by whom these actions are wrought, and with whom the Father and the Son are thus associated in glory and worship, must needs be none other than God over all, blessed for ever."

E. H. BICKERSTETH

THE DEITY OF THE SPIRIT

"The Holy Spirit of God."

Eph. 4:30

"The Lord who is the Spirit."

2 Cor. 3:18

"Go to Jordan and thou shalt see the Trinity", was an early Christian saying. The inauguration of our Lord's earthly ministry on the banks of the river Jordan, did indeed bring the three Persons of the Godhead strikingly to view.

> *"And Jesus, when He was baptized, went straightway up out of the water; and lo, the heavens were opened unto Him, and he saw the Spirit of God descending like a dove, and lighting upon Him. And lo, a voice from heaven saying, 'This is my beloved Son, in whom I am well pleased.' "*[1]

As the Spirit descended upon the Son in bodily form as a dove, the voice of the Father was heard identifying and authenticating His Son. By this association of Persons, the Holy Spirit is marked out not only as personal, but as divine. His deity is the necessary consequence of His personality, for the qualities attributed to His personality involve deity.

It is possible, however, while acknowledging the personality of the Spirit, to deny that He is a *divine* Person. Arius, the heretic from Alexandria, around whose teachings so much controversy raged, maintained that the Holy Spirit was a person, but denied His proper deity. According to him the Spirit is a created being, and if created, then not divine. The Nicene Creed, the formulation of which owed its origin in part to an endeavour to correct this error, speaks of the Holy Spirit as, "the Lord and giver of Life, Who proceedeth from the Father and the Son, Who with the Father and the Son together is worshipped and glorified, Who spake by the prophets". His deity is affirmed even more strongly in the Athanasian Creed: "The Father is God, the Son is God, the Holy Spirit is God. And yet there are not three Gods but one God."

When using the term divinity or deity of the Holy Spirit, we mean that He is divine, not merely as an emanation from the Father, but as being Himself God.

Evidence of His Godhead

We shall examine some of the lines of Scriptural evidence which support the claim of His eternal Godhead.

The names given to Him assert it. Deity is surely implied in His names, "Spirit of God", "Spirit of the Lord", "Spirit of our God",[2] "Spirit of your Father",[3] and many others. He is expressly called God in the record of the dissimulation of Ananias and Sapphira: "Why hath Satan filled thine heart to lie to the Holy Spirit? . . . Thou hast not lied unto men, but unto God."[4] The Holy Spirit and God are here identified as one.

His exercise of divine prerogatives supports it. Of the *Father* it is said, "Whatsoever the Lord pleased, that did He in heaven, and in earth, and in the seas."[5] Referring to His own sovereign power, the *Son* said, "All power is given unto me in heaven and in earth."[6] A like sovereignty is attributed to the *Holy Spirit* in His distribution of spiritual gifts. "All these worketh that one and the selfsame Spirit, dividing to each man severally as He will."[7]

Another significant and relevant passage occurs in the same chapter. "Now there are diversities of gifts, but the same *Spirit.* And there are differences of administrations, but the same *Lord.* And there are diversities of operations but it is the same God which worketh all in all."[8]

On this paragraph Meyer makes an illuminating comment: "The Divine Trinity is here indicated in an ascending climax in such a way that we pass from the Spirit Who bestows the gifts to the Lord (Christ) Who is served by means of them, and finally to God Who, as the absolute First Cause and Possessor of all Christian powers, works the entire sum of charismatic gifts in all who are gifted."

Ascription of Absolute Attributes

Attributes of deity ascribed to the Father and the Son are also predicated of the Spirit. These have been classified as *absolute,* those which inhere in the Divine essence, and *relative,* those in which He sustains relations to man and creation.

Reviewing first those which are inherent in His nature, we find *Eternity* is an attribute of God alone and indicates that He is uncreated. His self-offering was achieved through "the eternal

25

Spirit".[9] Then, too, He is "the Spirit of life",[10] which inheres in God alone. All other forms of life are derived. As both Father and Son have self-existent life,[11] so also has the Spirit, for "it is the Spirit that quickeneth".[12] He possesses also the attribute of *truth,* since He is not only "the Spirit of truth",[13] but "the Spirit is truth".[14] It is in virtue of this attribute that He is the medium of God's communication of truth, both in inspiration and illumination.

If it is true that "God is love", then this quality also must characterize the Holy Spirit if He is divine. It is not surprising, therefore, to find Paul using as a ground of appeal, "the *love* of the Spirit".[15]

As His name implies, holiness is the essence of His being. This, the attribute most frequently ascribed to Him, must be regarded as dominant, for it is really the sum-total of all His perfections. It is specifically ascribed to Him eighty-eight times, and is implicit in most of His other titles. Of the name "Holy Spirit", H. B. Swete writes: "The Spirit that is essentially, characteristically, uniquely holy; which being holy breathes the atmosphere of holiness into any spiritual nature that He enters and inhabits."

Ascription of Relative Attributes

Turning to those attributes that relate Him to others we learn that He is *omnipresent.* His presence in the universe is all-pervasive. "Whither shall I go from thy Spirit? or whither shall I flee from thy presence? If I ascend up into heaven, thou art there. If I take the wings of the morning and dwell in the uttermost part of the sea; even there shall thy hand lead me, and thy right hand shall hold me."[16] In the New Testament the words of our Lord carry a similar implication: "And I will pray the Father, and He shall give you another Comforter that He may abide with you forever."[17] If He is to abide with all the Lord's people simultaneously, He must be in all places simultaneously.

Omnipotence is also His prerogative—power adequate for all the stupendous requirements of creating and sustaining the universe. "In the beginning God created the heaven and the earth. . . . And the Spirit of God moved on the face of the waters.[18] His omnipotence is illustrated in His work which is likened to wind and water and fire. Of these symbols A. H. Strong writes: "The rushing mighty wind at Pentecost was the analogue of the wind-Spirit Who bore everything before Him on the first day of creation. The pouring out of the Spirit is likened to the flood of Noah when the windows of heaven were opened and there was not enough room to receive that which fell.[19] And the baptism of the Holy Spirit is like the fire that shall destroy all impurity at the end of the world."[20] Since He does that which omnipotence alone can do, He must be omnipotent.

His knowledge embraces infinity, for He is *omniscient*. Nothing can elude that knowledge. "The Spirit searches all things"— the whole reach of existence—"Yea the deep things of God",[21] and deity alone can fathom deity. If the Spirit knows all that God knows, then He possesses omniscience. Man is baffled by the judgments of God, they are unsearchable. But to the Spirit they are plain and open. Only because He knows all truth, is He able to guide us into all truth.

Our Lord's statement of the Spirit, "He will show you things to come",[22] implies that to Him the future is an open book. He is said to enjoy a knowledge that is possessed by God alone. "For what man knoweth the things of a man, save the spirit of man which is in him? Even so the things of God knoweth no man, but the Spirit of God."[23]

Subsidiary Proofs of Deity

His works attest His deity. Creation and conservation are the sole prerogatives of deity, and both are ascribed to the Holy Spirit.[24] Only a divine power could work such miracles as were performed through His agency. "I cast out devils by the Spirit of God,"[25] said Jesus. Even the lost legions of hell are conscious of and bow to His jurisdiction. The impartation of eternal life is in the power of God alone, and yet this is stated to be peculiarly the work of the Spirit. "Except a man be born of water and of the Spirit, he cannot enter the Kingdom of God."[26]

From *His co-ordinate rank with Father and Son* there emerges yet another proof of His Godhead. He is presented in association with them in terms of perfect equality at Christ's baptism, at the Pentecostal outpouring, in the apostolic commission and in the baptismal formula. The whole Trinity is represented as working in perfect unison for the accomplishment of man's redemption: "How much more shall the blood of *Christ* Who through the eternal *Spirit* offered Himself without spot to *God*, purge your conscience from dead works."[27]

The fact that *divine worship is paid to Him* affords a final evidence of His deity. We are baptized into the name (not names) of the Holy Spirit as well as of the Father and the Son.[28] The conjunction in one name of the Holy Three, forbids any other hypothesis than their equality and oneness. If one Person is to be worshipped, then all three are to be worshipped, for God is one.

So we conclude the Holy Spirit to be not only a real Person, but a divine Person, worthy of equal love, reverence and worship with the Father and the Son.

> *"O Holy Ghost, of sevenfold might,*
> *All graces come from Thee;*
> *Grant us to know and serve aright*
> *One God in Persons Three."*

REFERENCES

1. Matt. 3:16, 17. 2. Matt. 3:16, Luke 4:18, 1 Cor. 6:11. 3. Matt. 10:20. 4. Acts 5:3–4. 5. Psa. 135:6. 6. Matt. 28:18. 7. 1 Cor. 12:11. 8. 1 Cor. 12:4–6. 9. Heb. 9:14. 10. Rom. 8:2. 11. John 5:26: 12. John 6:63. 13. John 16:13. 14. 1 John 5:7 cf. John 14:16. 15. Rom. 15:13. 16. Psa. 139:7–10. 17. John 14:16–17. 18. Gen. 1:1, 2. 19. Mal. 3:10. 20. Matt. 3:11, 2 Pet. 3:7–13. 21. 1 Cor. 2:10. 22. John 16:13. 23. 1 Cor. 2:10, 11. 24. Job 26:13, Psa. 104:30. 25. Matt. 12:28. 26. John 3:5, Tit. 3:5. 27. Heb. 9:14. 28. Matt. 28:19.

Chapter Four

THE NAMES AND EMBLEMS
OF THE SPIRIT

"An examination of the Scriptural revelation on the Holy Spirit will indicate that He is nowhere assigned a formal name, such as we have for the Second Person, the Lord Jesus Christ, but is rather given descriptive titles, of which the most common in Scripture and in ordinary usage is the *Holy Spirit*. As His person is pure spirit, to which no material is essential, He is revealed in the Scriptures as the Spirit. The descriptive adjective *holy* is used to distinguish Him from other spirits which are creatures."

JOHN F. WALVOORD

"The Son of God was named by the angel before He was conceived in the womb: 'Thou shalt call His name Jesus, for He shall save His people from their sins.' Thus He came, not to receive a name, but to fulfil a name already predetermined for Him. In like manner was the Holy Ghost named by our Lord before His advent into the world: 'But when the Paraclete is come, Whom I will send unto you from the Father.' This designation of the Holy Spirit here occurs for the first time—a new name for the new ministry upon which He is now about to enter."

A. J. GORDON

THE NAMES AND EMBLEMS
OF THE SPIRIT

"The Spirit of Burning." Isa. 4:4

"The Spirit of Christ." Rom. 8:9

"The Spirit of truth." John. 14:17

It is a principle of Scripture that the names and emblems by which God has chosen to reveal Himself are intended to give insight into His true nature. An examination of these is, in consequence, a most important and instructive line of study. The many names assigned to the Holy Spirit are a divinely inspired commentary on His mission and work, and throw light upon His character. Even if we knew nothing more of Him than His names reveal, our conception would be rich indeed.

In the ninety passages in the Old Testament which directly refer to Him, eighteen different designations are employed. These fall roughly into three groups. (1) Those defining His relationship to God, e.g. "Spirit of God".[1] (2) Those defining His own character, e.g. "Holy Spirit".[2] (3) Those designating His operations on men, e.g. "Spirit of Wisdom".[3]

A much fuller and richer revelation of the Holy Spirit is to be found in the New Testament than in the Old, a fact reflected in the two hundred and fifty-four references to, and thirty-nine different designations of the Spirit. These titles (1) Express His relation to the Father and Son, e.g. "Spirit of your Father", and "Spirit of Christ".[4] (2) Affirm His own essential deity, e.g. "The Lord the Spirit".[5] (3) Reveal His own essential character, e.g. "Holy Spirit".[6] (4) Define His relation to those He has regenerated, e.g. "Spirit of Truth".[7]

Wind or Breath

His basic name, "Spirit", or "Spiritus", is the Latin synonym for the Greek "pneuma". Both words signify "breath" or "wind". Both thoughts are in the word as applied to the Holy Spirit. "He *breathed* on them and said, 'Receive ye the Holy Spirit'."[8] The thought here appears to be that He is the outbreathing of

God, His direct emanation, imparting His quickening life. When we receive the Spirit, we receive the inmost life of God to dwell in us.

The thought of *wind* also appears. "The wind bloweth where it listeth ... so is everyone that is born of the Spirit."[9] Here His operations are likened to the secrecy and sovereignty of the wind. The same association occurs in the account of the events on the Day of Pentecost. "There came a sound from heaven as of a rushing mighty wind, and it filled all the house where they were sitting, and they were all filled with the Holy Spirit."[10]

He is not named "Spirit" because He is spiritual in essence, for that may be similarly predicated of the Father and the Son. Nor has the adjective "Holy" special reference to His nature as being more holy than Father or Son. God is called "Holy Father". Jesus was called "Thy holy Child". He is no more holy than either of the other Persons of the Godhead. The word has reference to His official character, and conveys the thought of that He is Author of all holiness.

> *"And every virtue we possess,*
> *And every victory won,*
> *And every thought of holiness*
> *Are His alone."*

Of His many titles, three are selected as samples of a fruitful branch of Bible study.

He is called *"the Spirit of Christ"*.[11] A comparison of this verse with 1 Pet. 1:11 will demonstrate that it is not "a Christ-like spirit" that is here intended. Rather, that He is the gift of the ascended Christ whose office it is to reveal and glorify the One from Whom He proceeds. (John 7:37-39; 14:26; 16:14). He it is Who forms Christ spiritually in the Christian, as He formed Him physically in the Virgin's womb.[12]

Our Lord referred to Him as *"the Spirit of truth"*.[13] He is so called because it is His distinctive work to communicate and impart truth to us. All truth is from Him, and only as we subject ourselves to His teaching can He lead us into all truth. As Defender of truth, He is opposed to the "spirit of error".[14]

Christ Who was "full of grace and truth" is the reservoir of all grace, but it is the *"Spirit of Grace"*[15] Who administers and applies it. It is not only that He is gracious, but as the executive of the Godhead He confers grace. The grace of God which is always potentially ours, becomes ours in experience only as we receive it through the ministry of the Spirit of grace.

Emblems of the Spirit

It is in consonance with the revelation of the Third Person of the Trinity as "the seven Spirits which are before His throne",[16] that there are seven emblems employed to illustrate differing aspects of His Person and work. An emblem is "a picture representing to the mind something different from itself, a type or symbol". The sceptre, for example, is an emblem of sovereign power. A white robe is the emblem of purity.

The word "emblem" is so used when related to the Holy Spirit. To say that the Holy Spirit is like the wind is to express more than a thousand words could convey. Possibly this is the reason God has chosen to use so many emblems to illustrate what otherwise, because of the poverty of our language, we could never know.

Fire

In Isaiah's prophecy the Holy Spirit is referred to as "the Spirit of burning",[17] and of Christ it was prophesied "He shall baptize you in the Holy Spirit and in fire."[18] Here Spirit and fire are coupled with one preposition as a double baptism. As an emblem of the Spirit, fire, that mightiest and most terrible of human forces, represents primarily the *presence of the Triune God*. It appeared in the early dawn of history at Eden's gate, later at the burning bush, in the miraculous pillar of fire which attended Israel on her pilgrimage, in the fire from heaven which consumed the sacrifice. The climax of this representation was seen in the upper room when "cloven tongues like as of fire"[19] distributed themselves on the heads of the waiting disciples. Physical fire is not meant here, and so we look for results in the sphere of the supernatural and spiritual. These witnesses needed "tongues like as of fire" if they were to achieve their mission. The tongues of fire were symbols of aggressive Christianity. It would seem that this emblem refers to God's judicial presence as "the Spirit of judgment and the Spirit of burning".[20]

Fire symbolises also the *power of the Spirit*. The vision of the fiery tongues sitting on the heads of the disciples was emblematic of the universal gift of power to proclaim the evangel.[21] John contrasted the cold baptism of repentance received by his disciples, with the fiery baptism of power which the disciples of his Divine Successor would receive.[22] Just as the fiery sun is the source of power in the solar realm, so the Holy Spirit is the source of omnipotent power in the moral and spiritual realm. The fire of the Spirit produces burning zeal and incandescent love in the hearts of those wholly yielded to His influence. It resulted in unlearned and ignorant men turning the world upside down.

As the Spirit of burning, *His purifying influence* is in view. Since He is the Spirit of holiness, He cannot tolerate sin in the believer whose body is His temple. His purging work aims to consume from his heart everything that is out of harmony with His Divine nature.[23]

> "Come as the fire and purge our hearts
>   Like sacrificial flame,
> Let our whole soul an offering be
>   To our Redeemer's name."

Wind

The literal meaning of the Hebrew "ruach" and its Greek equivalent "pneuma" is "wind, breath, air". The Holy Spirit is referred to under this figure in three connections. *His vivifying power* is prominent in the vision of the valley of dry bones, when through His agency the dry bones were transformed into a mighty organized army.[24]

In the discourse with Nicodemus, it is *His regenerative work* which is compared to the unpredictable and irresistible motions of the wind.[25]

"The sound as of a rushing mighty wind" which accompanied the Spirit's descent, indicated *His mighty yet unseen power.* The wind was heard, but not felt, not a reality but a symbol. The literal translation would be, "a sound of a mighty blast borne along", an entirely supernatural sound and not due to ordinary physical phenomena. So is the working of the Spirit.

> "Come as the wind with rushing sound
>   And Pentecostal grace,
> That all of woman born may see
>   The glory of Thy face."

Water

This emblem pervades the typology of the Old Testament and the figurative language of the New. Its significance is varied; refreshment, fulness, satisfaction, cleansing, fructifying. Of all necessary things water seems the most indispensable. If water is so essential in the physical realm, it is yet more so in the spiritual.

Of many instructive passages, two especially merit attention. The first is the incident when Moses struck the rock in the wilderness, and from it there gushed a sparkling stream of water to slake the thirst of the Israelites.[26] Paul supplies the explanation of the symbolism in the statement, "and that Rock was Christ".[27] The water, life-giving and thirst-quenching was the Holy Spirit, poured out on the grounds of Christ's mediatorial work.

The second passage is from the prophet Ezekiel who saw a vision of a river emerging from beneath the threshold of the sanctuary.[28] Widening and deepening as it went, life and verdure sprang up wherever the river flowed, until it healed the deadly waters of the very sea in which it lost itself. The vision finds its interpretation in the words of our Lord spoken on "the last day, the great day of the feast" of Tabernacles. "He that believeth on me, as the Scripture hath said, from within him shall flow rivers of living water. But this spake he of the Spirit."[29]

While it is not explicitly stated that the Holy Spirit is the river, but only that this remark was made with reference to Him, He is nevertheless represented as the unfailing inner source from Whom outflowing streams of service and testimony proceed.

The cleansing properties of water are attributed to the Spirit in such passages as, "Then will I sprinkle clean water upon you, and ye shall be clean from all your filthiness and from all your idols will I cleanse you. . . . I will put my Spirit within you."[30] The divine cleansing is the necessary preparation for the divine indwelling.

Dove

This, the earliest symbol of the Holy Spirit,[31] recurs in each of the Gospels. The dove has been so considered in Christian art. Luke records that while Jesus was praying "the Holy Spirit descended in a bodily shape like a dove"[32] upon Him, thus establishing that gentle bird as an emblem of the Spirit. In the Talmud, Gen. 1:2 is rendered, "The Spirit of God, like a dove, brooded over the waters."

The traits of the dove strikingly exemplify several notable characteristics of the Spirit. Being a sacrificial bird it was of necessity "clean". It is very jealous of the purity of its plumage. It is said to have no gall and is certainly a lover of peace. The dove is especially fond of its home,[33] and mourns when deprived of the companionship of its mate.[34] Harmlessness is said to be characteristic of it.[35] From these considerations the appropriateness of the dove as a symbol of the Holy Spirit is readily seen.

> *"He came in semblance of a dove*
> *With sheltering wings outspread,*
> *The holy balm of peace and love,*
> *On us to shed."*

Seal

The Spirit is represented under the emblem of a seal in three passages: "In Whom having also believed, ye were sealed with the Holy Spirit."[36] "Grieve not the Holy Spirit of God where by ye are sealed."[37] "God hath also sealed us and given the earnest of the Spirit in our hearts."[38] This sealing is not some emotion or experience granted at some moment of high Christian experience. The seal is nothing less than the presence of God's Spirit in the believer.

The merchants of Ephesus, a maritime city, were familiar with the significance of the seal, as it was in constant use in commercial transactions. The Ephesians carried on an extensive timber trade. After selecting his timber, the merchant would stamp it with his own seal which was an accepted sign of ownership. He did not always carry off the timber at the time of purchase, but left it in the harbour with other floats of timber. But it was chosen, bought and sealed, awaiting only identification before being claimed and transported by the purchaser. Usually the merchant would send a trusted agent with his seal to identify the timber which bore a corresponding impress, and carry it away for his master's use. Even so the Holy Spirit impresses on the believer the image of Jesus Christ, and this is the sure pledge of the everlasting inheritance.

> *"Then on each He setteth*
> *His own secret sign;*
> *They that have my Spirit,*
> *These, saith He, are mine."*

Again, the emblem of the seal suggests rightful ownership, as when the farmer brands his cattle. "Having this seal, the Lord knoweth them that are His."[39]

The seal was used as the mark of genuineness of a legal document, a fact which led Paul to refer to his converts as the seal of his disputed apostleship. Among the Jews, sealing was the token of a completed contract. When the price had been paid, the

35

seal was attached to the contract to make it definite.[40] There is surely no clearer evidence of the finished transaction of Calvary, than the impartation of the Holy Spirit Who attests it.

As to the time of the sealing, the King James Version rendering is misleading, "*after that ye believed* ye were sealed".[41] These four words are a translation of one Greek word, "pisteusantes" which means, literally, "upon believing", or "having believed". While in order of salvation sealing follows believing, in order of time they come in one synchronous transaction.

Earnest

This word of Semitic origin is common in the papyri as earnest money in the purchase of a cow or a wife. In the New Testament it signifies part payment on a total obligation: "The Holy Spirit of promise, which is the *earnest* of our inheritance, unto the redemption of the purchased possession."[42]

In English law, "earnest" is a term denoting the payment of a sum of money to make a contract binding, guaranteeing a further payment to fulfil the contract. After a vendor has accepted the earnest or down-payment, he cannot refuse to carry out the terms of the contract. Of course the purchaser, too, has his obligations to fulfil.

It was the Hebrew custom for the vendor when agreeing to sell a piece of land, after receipt of the initial down-payment, to bind the bargain by giving the purchaser a handful of soil from the property he had bought. It was not only a receipt for the deposit, but actually part of his very purchase, the foretaste of possession of the whole.

God's initial gift of the Holy Spirit is a solemn guarantee and is like the first instalment of our inheritance, the assurance that our redemption will be fully carried out. It is the earnest and guarantee of a subsequent glorious fulness of the Spirit. This truth is helpfully presented in C. K. Williams' translation: "It is God Himself Who has made us ready for this change, and has given us the Spirit, a part payment and promise of more."[43]

Oil

This emblem appears in all the offerings of the priesthood and tabernacle. It occurs in the very name of Christ, but is not in every case a prefiguration of the work of the Spirit. The immediate references to the Spirit under the emblem of oil may be gathered from the five passages in which He is spoken of as the anointing. Three of these (Luke 4:18; Acts 4:27; 10:38), refer to the anointing of Jesus, and the other two (1 John 2:20, 27; 2 Cor. 1:21) refer to the Holy Spirit as a "chrisma", an anointing for the believer. The word means literally "an anointing", not the act of anointing, but that with which it is performed. When Christ, the Lord's Anointed was about to commence His public ministry, at His baptism He was anointed not with oil but with the Holy Spirit.[44] It would seem, therefore, that the anointing we have received from God, is the same Holy Spirit: "But ye have an unction from the Holy One, and ye know all things."[45] Every believer is a king and priest unto God, set apart by the anointing received at regeneration.

In the Old Testament it was oil alone that lighted the temple "where God's honour dwells", and where the Person of Christ was so fully symbolized. In a similar manner the Spirit illuminates Christ to us. As oil is the source of light,[46] so is the Spirit the constant source of effective witness to Christ.

Oil is the emblem of gladness, for it was said of the Anointed One, "God hath anointed Thee with the oil of gladness above Thy fellows."[47] And is not joy and gladness the fruit of the Spirit?

> *"Thou the anointing Spirit art,*
> *Who dost Thy sevenfold gifts impart,*
> *Thy blessed unction from above*
> *In comfort, life and fire of love."*

REFERENCES

1. Isa. 11:2. 2. Psa. 57:11. 3. Isa. 11:2. 4. Matt. 10:20, Rom. 8:9. 5. 2 Cor. 3:18. 6. Matt. 1:18. 7. John 14:17. 8. John 20:22. 9. John 3:8. 10. Acts 2:2, 4. 11. Rom. 8:9. 12. Gal. 4:19. 13. John 14:17. 14. John 4:6. 15. Heb. 10:29. 16. Rev. 1:4. 17. Isa. 4:4. 18. Matt. 3:11. 19. Acts 2:3. 20. Isa. 4:4. 21. Act 1:8 cf. 2:3. 22. Matt. 3:11. 23. Mal. 3:3, Heb. 12:29. 24. Ezek. 37:7–10. 25. John 3:3–8. 26. Exod. 17:6. 27. 1 Cor. 10:4. 28. Ezek. 47:1. 29. John 7:37–39. 30. Ezek. 36:25, 27. 31. Gen. 1:2. 32. Luke 3:22. 33. Isa. 60:8. 34. Isa. 38:14. 35. Matt. 10:16. 36. Eph. 1:13. 37. Eph. 4:30. 38. 2 Cor. 1:22. 39. 2 Tim. 2:19. 40. Jer. 32:9–10. 41. Eph. 1:13. 42. Eph. 1:13, 14. 43. 2 Cor. 5:5. 44. Luke 4:18 cf. Isa. 61:1. 45. 1 John 2:20. 46. Exod. 25:6. 47. Heb. 1:9.

Chapter Five

THE THREEFOLD CONVICTION
OF THE SPIRIT

"This threefold work of the Spirit is further defined in the passage which follows. The work of convicting or convincing the world of sin is given the specific character of revealing the one sin of unbelief as being the issue between the unsaved and God ... Because of the death of Christ it is no longer a question of being condemned simply because of sin. The death of Christ is seen to satisfy all the righteous demands of God. To the unsaved the determining factor in his destiny is whether he believes in Christ."

JOHN F. WALVOORD

"As to the nature of that convincing influence which the Spirit brings to bear upon the mind, several things come under our consideration. He sets forth truth to the mind, and maintains it against prepossession or contrary opinion. The Holy Spirit, by the word alone, or through the ministry of those who preach it, convinces the unbelieving world, by the prophecies of the Old Testament—by the testimonies of the New Testament—so fitly and seasonably, that the unwilling are made willing, and compelled to feel and to admit in their conscience the truth of the Gospel—an impression which is followed by faith in the heart and confession with the mouth. They are pressed by the force of truth, and yield."

"More particularly, He convinces the mind in a threefold way, viz. that unbelief is the greatest sin; that the righteousness procured by Christ is the only righteousness which avails before God; and that all the right or claim which Satan had to the possession of man, once his captive but now redeemed, is so invalidated, because the process has been decided against him, that he cannot tyrannize over any but by their own will."

GEORGE SMEATON

THE THREEFOLD CONVICTION
OF THE SPIRIT

"Nevertheless I tell you the truth: it is to your advantage that I go away, for if I do not go away, the Counselor will not come to you; but if I go, I will send Him to you. And when He comes, He will convince the world of sin and of righteousness and of judgment: of sin, because they do not believe in me; of righteousness, because I go to the Father, and you will see me no more; of judgment, because the ruler of this world is judged."

John 16:7-11 (RSV)

"When He is come" is a recurring clause which sheds helpful light on three aspects of the ministry of the Spirit. When He comes He will reveal the sufficiency of Christ,[1] the certainty of truth[2] and the sinfulness of sin.[3] It is with the last aspect that this pregnant paragraph is concerned. Before the descent of the Spirit at Pentecost, the world was blind to its sin and need. With His advent moral issues were gradually clarified and men began to take sin seriously.

The word "reprove" used here is translated also "convince" or "convict". Perhaps a combination of these two words is required to render its exact sense. It is a legal term signifying the presentation of evidence that conveys with it the proof of wrongdoing. J. H. Moulton defines it as a bringing to light of the true character of the man and his conduct. Bishop Westcott points out that the word has four shades of meaning which should be borne in mind in studying the theme: (1) An authoritative examination of the facts. (2) Unquestionable proof. (3) Decisive judgment. (4) Punitive power. "When He is come", all these elements are present in His conviction. The "world" of which He spoke was of course, the world of men, mankind alienated from God and opposed to Him.

The Spirit's threefold conviction may be summarized: There is such a thing as *sin*, and its essence is the refusal to believe on Christ. There is such a thing as *righteousness* and it was embodied in the Incarnate Christ, and attested by His return to heaven. There is such a thing as *judgment*, which consists in the

40

triumph through Christ of righteousness over sin and Satan. We consider first

The Gravity of Sin

"He will convict the world of sin ... because they believe not on me."

A jury may convict of crimes; conscience may convict of sins; but only the Spirit of God can convict of sin. It is of sin in the singular that the Spirit convicts. Of which sin? Murder? Adultery? Theft? Lying? When a man commits such sins his own natural conscience will accuse him, unless it is seared. That requires no special conviction of the Spirit. To the world sin is an outward act, the breach of some law which is unfortunate but not necessarily culpable, so long as it does not outrage local conventions.

"I don't see why God should be so hard on my peccadilloes" said a man of the world. His outlook is characteristic. Christ's definition of sin differs radically from that of society or even from the usual theological formulae. He goes straight to the very heart of sin and affirms that the primary mission of the Paraclete is to convince unregenerate men that the one damning sin is failure to believe in Himself. Sin became a new thing with His advent: "If I had not come and spoken unto them, they had not had sin; but now they have no cloke for their sin."[4]

To the man of the world, unbelief in Christ seems a trifling matter, and out of all proportion to the magnitude of the results the Scriptures say accrue from it. Nor will he ever realize the gravity, the exceeding sinfulness of this crucial sin except by the Spirit's illumination.

Trivial though it may seem, unbelief is the parent of all sin, and the Spirit will present to the heart incontrovertible evidence that this is so. The reception and embracing of this evidence will lead to eternal life, but rejected and refused it leads to inevitable judgment. The Holy Spirit reveals Christ as a Saviour Who must be received or rejected.

On the day of Pentecost, the Spirit engaged in this convicting work. He enlightened the minds of the assembled crowds to one sin of commanding importance—that of rejecting and crucifying Christ. "Him ... ye have taken and by wicked hands have crucified and slain ... know assuredly that God hath made that same Jesus whom ye have crucified both Lord and Christ. Now when they heard this, they were pricked in their hearts and said ... what shall we do?"[5]

41

Enlightened by the Spirit, they were now prepared to admit that "wicked hands" had nailed Jesus to the cross. The truths proclaimed by Peter which produced such astounding results were these three—sin, righteousness and judgment. He charged the house of Israel with the *sin* of rejecting Christ. He proclaimed the *righteousness* of Christ, "a man approved of God", which was attested by His exaltation to God's right hand. He announced the fact of *judgment;* "until I make thine enemies my footstool".

These are the truths the Holy Spirit uses to the conversion of sinful men. "They were pricked in their hearts ... then they that gladly received His word were baptized."

After a service, a young woman approached Dr. H. A. Ironside: "I don't like the way you put things. You made me feel very uncomfortable tonight. I have never knowingly done a wicked thing. I am respected by all my friends. No one can say a word against my character. The only thing you yourself could object to is that I do not belong to any church, or care anything about Jesus Christ; and yet you class me with people who are living wickedly."

"Suppose you came and told me something like this," he replied. " 'I have always been good and respectable. Nobody can say anything against me, except that though I have the best mother in the world, I do not care anything about her. I am utterly indifferent to her'. What would you expect me to think of you?"

"Oh", she exclaimed, "I could not be a good girl and not love my mother."

"Well", he replied, "I told you tonight of One Who has loved you with a love such as no mother ever knew; One Who for your sake gave Himself to save you from a danger your finite mind cannot realize, and Who now asks your trust and confidence, and you say you care nothing for Him. What do you think God thinks of such indifference to His Son?"

She hung her head and said, "I never thought of it like that." A few nights later she confessed Christ as her Lord and Saviour.

Such is the Spirit's conviction of sin. But it is of small comfort to a troubled heart to be convicted of sin, unless he is also assured that there is available to him a righteousness adequate to meet his now conscious and desperate need.

The Possibility of Righteousness

"He will convict the world of righteousness ... because I go to the Father."

42

The overwhelming consciousness of sin such as gripped the crowd on the day of Pentecost, this startling revelation of his own unrighteousness, might well drive the now penitent man to despair. But it is at this point that the Holy Spirit draws his attention to the exalted Christ, and convinces him that there is available to him a righteousness that is not his own.[6]

In the courts of law when a man is convicted of wrong-doing, the next step is judgment. If a man has embezzled his employer's money, he is tried, found guilty and convicted. What comes next? Judgment is pronounced and he bears the penalty.

But God is very gracious. He arrests the processes of the law, and interpolates another process unknown to the law courts. "He will convict the world of righteousness."

The world's conception of righteousness is as faulty as its conception of sin. The unregenerate man is totally ignorant of the true nature of righteousness. He is perfectly satisfied with the belief that "his creed is right whose life is in the right". Morality or external presentability is the nearest approach to righteousness with which he is familiar, but uncover his deepest heart, and you will find there a nest of unsuspected things.

Man's righteousness is the result of doing his best, or "the works of the law", as Paul puts it. It is the Spirit's function to correct these false and superficial views of righteousness, by directing attention to Christ glorified. He convinces the newly awakened soul that "now, apart from the law, a righteousness of God hath been manifested ... even the righteousness of God through faith in Jesus Christ unto all them that believe".[7]

Where is this righteousness found? In "Jehovah Tsidkenu", the Lord our righteousness. Robert Murray McCheyne told of his discovery in these words:

> "When free grace awoke me by light from on high,
> Then legal fears shook me, I trembled to die;
> No refuge, no safety, in self could I see,
> 'Jehovah Tsidkenu' my Saviour must be."

This righteousness is not in the abstract, but is incarnated in His own Person and exhibited in His character and work. Until God set His seal of acceptance on Christ's expiatory work, there was no righteousness available for sinning men. But now the exalted Christ has perfected a righteousness that is freely given to all who believe.

Was it not expedient for us that He went away and sent the Holy Spirit to represent Him on earth? So long as the High Priest was within the veil, Israel had no assurance of their acceptance with God. Christ has entered into the holiest of all for us, and will emerge only at the Second Advent. How then can we be assured that we have a righteousness acceptable to God? He has sent His Spirit to bear witness of that fact in our hearts. "The presence of the Spirit in the midst of the Church, is the proof of the presence of Christ in the midst of the throne."

The Certainty of Judgment

"He will convict the world of judgment . . . because the prince of this world hath been judged."

This verse is frequently misquoted, and consequently often misunderstood. It is often quoted as: "He will convict the world of judgment *to come.*" But that is not what it says or means. When Paul reasoned with Felix, his theme was "righteousness, temperance and judgment to come", but the Spirit's conviction is of a judgment that is already *past.* "The prince of this world *hath been* judged."

Who is the prince of this world? None other than Satan, the Devil, the Usurper. The common conception of this powerful personage is coloured more by the lurid conceptions of Dante and Milton than by Holy Writ, but that he has great power over men is abundantly clear from Scripture.

Satan has always been in conflict with righteousness, and never more so than when it was incarnate in Jesus Christ the righteous. In his *Nativity Ode,* Milton graphically depicts the effects of the incarnation on the Devil:

> *"From this happy day*
> *The old dragon underground,*
> *In straiter limits bound,*
> *Not half so far casts his usurped sway:*
> *And wroth to see his Kingdom fail:*
> *Swinges the scaly horror of his folded tail."*

Satan used Herod's political ambitions and fear of a rival, to attempt the destruction of the new-born King. In the lonely wilderness he launched an all-out attack through every avenue of His human nature, tempting Him through appetite and avarice and ambition. Thwarted in every attempt, the Enemy gathered all his forces and hurled them against the prostrate Son of God in the Garden of Gethsemane in an endeavour to destroy Him before ever he reached Golgotha. Here too he was ignominiously defeated.

The final conflict was staged on Calvary's hill. To see Jesus hanging there dead, would make it appear that *He* had been judged, and the prince of this world was victorious. The resurrection proved that in reality, it was not Christ but the rebel Prince who had been judged. True, Satan bruised His heel, but the Seed of the woman mortally wounded his head, a wound from which he will never recover. "Through death he destroyed him that hath the power of death, that is the devil."[8] It was a victory open to all: "He rid himself of all the Powers of evil, and held them up to open contempt, when he celebrated his triumph over them on the cross."[9]

From that hour of triumph, Satan has been judged, under sentence, vanquished. To us, Satan's judgment seems to be a process still going on. To the Son of God it is already accomplished, "the prince of this world hath been judged". On the return of the Seventy from their successful preaching tour, Jesus exclaimed, "I beheld Satan fall as lightning from heaven".[10] With omniscient vision, He had already seen Satan fall, like a flash of lightning. He had already heard the clanking of his chains as he was cast into the lake of fire.

Although the judgment has not yet been finally executed, it is as certain as though it were. John's graphic description of the conflict between Christ and Satan and its inevitable issue affords a heartening prospect:

"And there was war in heaven: Michael and his angels fought against the dragon; and the dragon fought and his angels, And prevailed not; neither was their place found any more in heaven. And the great dragon was cast out, that old serpent, called the Devil, and Satan, which deceiveth the whole world: he was cast out into the earth, and his angels were cast out with him."[11]

"And the devil that deceived them was cast into the lake of fire and brimstone, where the beast and the false prophet are, and shall be tormented day and night for ever and ever."[12]

True to His trust, the Spirit of truth convinces the repentant and now believing heart that it, too, will see Satan fall as lightning from heaven, since Christ has judged the whole Kingdom of evil. Because He overcame Satan, the weakest believers may share His triumph, and "overcome him by the blood of the Lamb and by the word of their testimony."[13]

The choice for men today is crystal clear. They must either embrace God's righteousness in Christ, or throw in their lot with a doomed world. To do the latter means to share its doom. To do the former means to share His victory.

REFERENCES

1. John 15:26, 16:14. 2. John 16:13. 3. John 16:8. 4. John 15:22. 5. Acts 2:23, 36, 37. 6. Rom. 10:3. 7. Rom. 3:21, 22 RV. 8. Heb. 2:14. 9. Col. 2:15 TCNT. 10. Luke 10:18. 11. Rev. 12:7–9. 12. Rev. 20:10 TCNT. 13. Rev. 12:11.

Chapter Six

THE SIGNIFICANCE OF
PENTECOST

"Pentecost is a prophecy of the universal proclamation of the Gospel, and of the universal praise which shall one day rise to Him that was slain. This company of brethren praising God in the tongues of the whole world represented the whole world which shall one day praise God in its various tongues."

"Pentecost prophesied of the time when 'men of every tribe and tongue, and people, and nation' should lift up their voices to Him who has purchased them unto God with His blood. It began a communication of the Spirit to all believers which is never to cease while the world stands. The mighty rushing sound has died into silence, the fiery tongues rest on no heads now, the miraculous results of the gifts of the Spirit have passed away also, but the gift remains, and the Spirit of God abides for ever with the Church of Christ."

ALEXANDER MACLAREN

"Just as the feast of the Passover found its fulfilment on the day of the Saviour's crucifixion, so the feast of the firstfruits found its fulfilment on the day of Pentecost. It remains only for the feast of Tabernacles to be fulfilled at our Lord's second coming, when the harvest of the earth shall have been completely gathered in."

"We should notice also the perfect agreement here of type with antitype. Our Saviour as the Lamb of God, died on the cross, and so fulfilled the meaning of the Paschal feast. On the morrow after the Paschal Sabbath, i.e. on Easter Sunday, He arose again, in exact conformity with the type, as the 'sheaf of firstfruits.' On the fiftieth day after the presentation of that resurrection sheaf, the first fruits of the harvest were gathered in upon the day of Pentecost."

THOMAS WALKER

THE SIGNIFICANCE OF PENTECOST

"When the day of Pentecost was fully come...
they were all filled with the Holy Spirit."

Acts 2:1, 4.

Pentecost is second only to Calvary in importance to the Christian, for Pentecost is the complement of Calvary. Without Pentecost, Calvary would have been ineffective to redeem lost mankind. It required the dynamic of the Spirit as well as the sacrifice of the Saviour to bring the benefits of salvation to a waiting world, for all Christian experience revolves around the twin centres of Calvary and Pentecost. Calvary opened the fountain from which all the blessings of Pentecost flowed. Pentecost made available to men all that Calvary made possible.

Had Pentecost been omitted from the Divine counsels, it would have been like perfecting a costly machine, and then failing to supply it with the necessary motive power. Pentecost is the power-house of Christianity. Not until the descent of the Spirit on that memorable day, was the throb of power heard in the machinery God had perfected for man's redemption.

The appropriateness of the day of Pentecost for the descent of the Holy Spirit is obvious.[1] A cosmopolitan assembly had gathered in Jerusalem for the feast, providing a unique occasion for the first large-scale dissemination of the gospel. It was the "feast of firstfruits,"[2] and thus singularly fitting for the garnering and presentation to the Head of the Church of the three thousand, firstfruits of the greater harvest to follow. To the Jews, the feast marked their deliverance from their Egyptian bondage, and illustrated the liberating ministry of the Spirit.[3]

Augustine designated the day of Pentecost *the dies natalis of the Holy Spirit,* a conception quite in harmony with Scripture. At the dawn of human history, God the Father visited earth for the purpose of man's creation.[4] Several millenniums later came another celestial Visitor, this time in the person of the Son, to accomplish man's redemption. On the day of Pentecost the Third Person of the Trinity, the Holy Spirit came to earth to achieve man's regeneration and to fit him for life as a child of God.

48

The Preparation

The statement, "when the day of Pentecost was fully come", or better, "was being fulfilled", implied that preparation had been going on, as indeed it had been. Pentecost was the logical outcome of all the activities of the Godhead since the fall of man. It was the culmination of a preparation extending over millenniums.

This preparation began with the first prophecy in Scripture— God's sentence on the Serpent: "I will put enmity between thee and the woman, and between thy seed and her seed; it shall bruise thy head and he shall bruise thy heel."[5] Frequently in the Old Testament the prophets prepare the way for the advent of the Spirit: "I will pour out my Spirit upon all flesh."[6] "I will put my Spirit within you."[7]

With the advent of Christ, the preparation became more apparent. In His earlier ministry references to the Spirit are few, but as He drew near to the close of His time on earth, this theme became increasingly prominent in His teaching. He began to prepare the minds of the disciples for the fulfilment of the prophecies, and to recognize the fulfilment when it came.

As the promised day drew near, Jesus counselled His disciples to tarry in Jerusalem until they were endued with power from on high.[8] Their hearts must be prepared for the reception of the gift of the Spirit, and this was effectively achieved during the ten-day prayer meeting in the upper room. The prayer meeting did not cause the descent of the Spirit, but it brought the waiting believers into a condition in which they were ready to welcome the heavenly Guest into their hearts.

It is not difficult to imagine the humbling they experienced and the intense yearning for the promised blessing that gripped their hearts. They would be overwhelmed with a sense of inadequacy for the task their Lord had entrusted to them, nothing less than the evangelization of the world. Old Scriptures began to glow with new meaning. With what fresh illumination Joel's prophecy would come to their hearts: "It shall come to pass afterward, that I will pour out my Spirit upon all flesh. . . . Upon the servants and the handmaids in that day I will pour out my Spirit."[9] With cleansed, palpitating hearts they waited for the promise of the Father.

The Advent

The narrative thrills with life and power.

"And when the day of Pentecost was fully come, they were all with one accord in one place. And suddenly there came a sound from heaven as of a rushing mighty wind, and it filled all the house where they were sitting. And there appeared unto them cloven tongues like as of fire, and it sat upon each of them. And they were all filled with the Holy Ghost, and began to speak with other tongues, as the Spirit gave them utterance."

Acts 2 : 1–4

The audible sound "as of a mighty blast"—no motion in the air, yet a sound like the raging of a hurricane. *The visible sign,* "cloven tongues like as of fire" distributing themselves on the heads of the worshippers. It happened suddenly. It came "from heaven", a blessing from the very throne of God. No merely natural phenomenon this, for it was not physical wind or fire with natural physical effects. We are face to face with the sphere of the spiritual and supernatural. And all this was preparatory to the advent of *the Indwelling Guest:* "They were all filled with the Holy Spirit," Who took full possession of their redeemed personalities.

Why wind and fire? These are nature's most powerful and yet most devastating agents. The sound of the wind was not of a gentle zephyr but of a raging tornado, to awe them with its irresistible power. Fire can be terrifying in its devastating fury, yet beneficent when its laws are observed. He Who had come in their midst was "awful in holiness", yet His ministry was to be benevolent.

There was no room for doubt that the promised Comforter had come. Wondering eyes and throbbing heart alike testified to His majestic presence. The wind that "bloweth where it listeth" and "the Spirit of burning" had fallen on the one hundred and twenty expectant hearts. By this mighty baptism He fused them into one. So filled with ecstasy were they that their other-worldly joy was mistaken for drunkenness. The only explanation that seemed to fit the case was, "These men are filled with new wine".

With the irresistible influx of the Divine life, barriers were broken down, and, borne along by the Fiery Spirit they began to speak with other tongues—*the reversal of Babel.* There their *language* was confounded, one tongue became many, and the apostate race was scattered over the face of the earth. Here *they* were confounded, for they heard many languages as one. "Every man heard them speak in his own language the wonderful works of God."

The Significance

"What meaneth this?",[10] is always the question of the crowd that gathers where something exciting is happening.

First, this outpouring of the Spirit was *God's seal on the Messiahship of Jesus,* and the fulfilment of His promise. It was the vindication of Christ to the Jews, a signal reversal of their condemnation and rejection of His Son.

Then it was the occasion of *the institution of the Church* as a living, irresistible organism. While the Church doubtless had its genesis where the two disciples left John the Baptist and followed Jesus, it was not until the day of Pentecost that it became an organic entity. Spontaneously and without human organization the Church came into being.

Again, Pentecost meant *the influx of a new power* into the life of the disciples, for the discharge of new responsibilities. "The descent of the Holy Spirit on the disciples at Pentecost," says H. B. Swete, "was to them what the descent of the Holy Spirit upon our Lord at His baptism was to Him. It was *their initiation into an official ministry.* As in His instance, so too in theirs, it occurred on the threshold of public responsibility."

As in apostolic times, manifestations of the divine power will follow in the wake of a similar filling of the Holy Spirit. In recounting his visit to meetings conducted in China by Dr. Jonathan Goforth, Rev. Walter Philips supplies us with contemporary evidence that the power of Pentecost is operative in our day.

"At once, on entering the church, one was conscious of something unusual. The place was crowded to the door, and tense, reverent attention sat on every face. The very singing was vibrant with new joy and vigour.... The people knelt for prayer, silent at first, but soon one here and another there began to pray aloud. The voices grew and gathered volume and blended into a great wave of united supplication that swelled till it was almost a roar, and died down again into an undertone of weeping. Now I understood why the floor was so wet—it was wet with pools of tears! The very air seemed electric—I speak in all seriousness —and strange thrills coursed up and down one's body.

"Then above the sobbing, in strained, choking tones, a man began to make public confession. Words of mine will fail to describe the awe and terror and pity of these confessions. It was not so much the enormity of the sins disclosed, or the depths of iniquity sounded, that shocked one.... It was the agony of the penitent, his groans and cries, and voice shaken with sobs; it was the sight of men forced to their feet, and in spite of their struggles, impelled, as it seemed, to lay bare their hearts, that moved one and brought the smarting tears to one's own eyes. Never have I experienced anything more heart-breaking, more nerve-racking than the spectacle of those souls stripped naked before their fellows."

The Transformation

Of all the marvels accompanying the effusion of the Spirit at Pentecost, none is greater than the change effected in the disciples themselves. They had been meeting behind closed doors for fear of the Jews. Now shrinking timidity gives place to *lion-like boldness*. Peter the denier is unrecognizable in the fearless preacher who faces the rulers of the Jews and charges them with their guilt.[11] All fear seems to have been consumed by the baptism of fire. Nor was Peter alone in this. His companions exhibited the same spirit. The indwelling Guest had worked this tremendous transformation.

In the American Civil War, Sheridan's army was attacked in his absence. The camp was routed. Men threw down their arms and fled like scared sheep. Suddenly they stopped, formed, turned, and drove back their foes, capturing their artillery. What had happened to turn frightened sheep into conquering warriors, and a disgraceful rout into a glorious victory? General Sheridan had suddenly ridden into their midst, and immediately his conquering personality passed into the men and they were changed. In like manner were the disciples changed by the promised advent of the Victorious Christ into their midst in the person of His Spirit.

A second marvel was the *spontaneous joy* which welled up in their hearts, "joy in the Holy Spirit". There is nothing so attractive, nothing that so arouses wistfulness in the hearts of men and women of the world as true Christian joy. At a loss to account for it, the Jews attributed it to intoxication. Peter identified it as coming, not from wine but from the Holy Spirit, the Divine Stimulus.

These were indeed God-intoxicated men. The observers were nearer the truth than they knew, for there are some striking correspondences between the stimulation of wine and the stimulus of the Holy Spirit. Wine stimulates the sluggish, exhilarates the pessimistic, emboldens the fearful, loosens the tongue of the inarticulate.

The Extent

Peter, illuminated by the Spirit, identified the events of this memorable day with the prophecy of Joel: "I will pour out of my Spirit upon all flesh: and your sons and your daughters shall prophesy, and your young men shall see visions, and your old men shall dream dreams; and on my servants and on my handmaidens I will pour out in those days of my Spirit..."[12]

"Ye shall receive the gift of the Holy Spirit, for the promise is unto you, and to your children, and to all that are afar off, even as many as the Lord our God shall call."[13]

Could a more comprehensive promise be made? It is not for a spiritual elite. All, irrespective of sex, race or rank are eligible to receive it.

The Achievement

And what of the impact of these changed men on the hostile Jews and the unbelieving world? Of Stephen it was said, "They were not able to resist the wisdom and the power by which he spoke."[14] "These men which have turned the world upside down are come here also."[15]

Note the accessions to the ranks of these "ignorant and unlearned men".[16] "Three thousand souls."[17] "About five thousand."[18] "Multitudes, both of men and women."[19] "The number of the disciples was multiplied."[20] "A great company of priests were obedient to the faith."[21] Such was the effect of the tongue of fire. The church grew, not by addition, but by multiplication.

Before long, in accordance with the Lord's prediction and through the Spirit's working, the circle of their influence widened, and Samaria was included.[22] Once prejudice was overcome, a mighty revival swept the area under the preaching of Philip.

A little later the Spirit overcame Peter's Jewish scrupulousness and exclusiveness,[23] and through him the door of faith was opened to the Gentiles.[24] The assembled company in the house of Cornelius experienced a like baptism to that enjoyed by the disciples on the day of Pentecost.

The implication of this great historical event which was also the foreshadowing of a possible present experience, will be discussed in subsequent chapters.

"Lord God the Holy Ghost,
In this accepted hour,

As on the day of Pentecost,
Descend in all Thy power.

"Like rushing, mighty wind
Upon the waves beneath,
Move with one impulse every mind,
One soul, one feeling breathe.

"The young, the old inspire
With wisdom from above,
And give us hearts and tongues of fire
To pray and praise and love."

REFERENCES

1. Acts 2:8–11. 2. Lev. 23:17. 3. 2 Cor. 3:17. 4. Gen. 1:27.
5. Gen. 3:15. 6. Joel 2:28. 7. Ezek. 36:27. 8. Luke 24:49.
9. Joel 2:28, 29. 10. Acts 2:12. 11. Acts 2:23. 12. Acts 2:17,
18. 13. Acts 2:39. 14. Acts 6:10. 15. Acts 17:6. 16. Acts 4:13.
17. Acts 4:13. 18. Acts 4:4. 19. Acts 5:14. 20. Acts 6:1.
21. Acts 6:7. 22. Acts 8:6. 23. Acts 10:44, 45. 24. Acts 14:27.

Chapter Seven

THE SPIRIT IN THE BELIEVER

"More particularly, the Holy Spirit works in the process of sanctification by producing in the soul those special virtues which may be lacking in particular persons, or needed on particular occasions. One Christian, for example, may be constitutionally defective in courage, another in meekness, another in patience, and so on. These special qualities the Spirit of God can and does bestow; as Paul reminds Timothy, who seems to have been of a naturally timid and shrinking disposition, 'God gave us not a spirit of fearfulness, but of power, and of love, and of discipline'; or as the fiery spirit of the son of thunder was chastened and refined, so that he became the Apostle of love. There are special aspects of God's revelation in Christ fitted to draw forth special virtues, and to discourage and check the faults opposed to them; and these the Holy Spirit uses for these ends; as we may see how Paul's second letter to Timothy sets forth those views of Christian truth and experience that are most likely to encourage and strengthen a timid disciple. The trials and afflictions of life, too, are made the means of promoting and perfecting in believers virtues in which they may be defective . . . All these virtues are described as the fruit of the Spirit, and are wrought and maintained by the Spirit in the heart."

J. S. CANDLISH

"There can be no holiness without the truth of God, and there can be no holiness without the Spirit's guidance in that truth. When we speak of Divine guidance we think simply of being safely led through the events and circumstances of daily life. There is a higher guidance than that. People go astray in act because they go astray in thought. Wrong thinking is the beginning of all wrong action. To know the truth is to think aright, and thinking aright is the secret of acting aright, and the Holy Spirit is sent to minister the truth, that we may think aright."

EVAN H. HOPKINS

THE SPIRIT IN THE BELIEVER

"Born of the Spirit"   John 3:5.

"The ... Spirit ... hath made me free"   Rom. 8:2

"Sanctification of the Spirit"   2 Thess. 2:13.

It is impossible within the limits of space available to treat all the Spirit's ministries in the life of the Christian, but we shall consider some of them.

Regeneration—born of the Spirit

A previous chapter describes the work of the Spirit in conviction of sin in the heart of the non-Christian, a necessary preliminary to repentance and the imparting of the divine nature. Only one who has been convicted in this way is prepared for the positive work of the Spirit.

The new birth is the *sine qua non* of entry into the Church. "Except a man be born again he cannot see the Kingdom of God."[1] No advantages of birth, culture or religion can make regeneration unnecessary. Apart from it, all men are "dead through their trespasses and sins."[2] On repentance and faith, however, the Spirit imparts eternal life to the one who was spiritually dead.

It is not fanning into flame an already existent divine spark, for no such spark exists. Nor does He lift the natural life to a higher plane, for "that which is born of the flesh is flesh, and that which is born of the Spirit is spirit".[3] His method is a new creation, not mere reformation.[4] Incredible though it seems, He makes the now believing soul a "partaker of the Divine nature"[5]— the very nature of God. At the moment of believing he receives eternal life.[6]

The Word of God is the instrument He uses to achieve regeneration: "Being born again, not of corruptible seed, but of incorruptible, by the Word of God which liveth and abideth for ever."[7] The good seed of the Word is sown in the soil of the prepared heart, and quickened by the Spirit, germinates into life. Without the Spirit there could be no such thing as a Christian, for "no man can say that Jesus Christ is Lord but by the Holy Spirit".

Emancipation—freed from sin.

Not content with imparting this new life, the Holy Spirit emancipates the new man from the domination of sin. "The law of the Spirit of life in Christ Jesus *hath made me free* from the law of sin and death."

This truth is almost as revolutionary as that of regeneration. Comparatively few Christians either know or believe that Christ's death and resurrection made deliverance from the power of indwelling sin possible. Nor do they know that the Spirit is waiting to make this deliverance an actual fact in their experience. Three times over in Romans 6 Paul repeats three glorious words, "free from sin"—emancipation, and holds them out as the right of every believer.

In this verse, two opposing laws are mentioned operating in the Christian's heart. The stronger of these is said to emancipate the Christian from the power of the weaker.

I have in my hand a piece of lead. I hold it over a pool of water, and relax my grip. The lead is drawn irresistibly earthwards and sinks to the bottom of the pool. It has been mastered by the law of gravitation. I take the same piece of lead, attach it to a piece of wood and drop it into the pool. Now it floats. No change has taken place in the nature or tendency of the lead, nor has the law of gravitation ceased to function, but through its union with the wood, it has been mastered by a stronger law, the law governing floating bodies, and has been emancipated from the downward pull of gravitation.

In our natural state, we are mastered by the law of sin and death. We are at the mercy of its downward pull. But after regeneration, by virtue of our union with Christ and the indwelling of His Spirit, the irresistible "law of the Spirit of life" is on our side, and we are now no longer captives under the tyranny of the law of sin and death. This potential freedom becomes actual when it is appropriated by faith. The formula which brings this powerful law into the field of our need is given by Paul: "Reckon ye yourselves to be *dead* indeed unto sin"— because our old sinful self was crucified with Christ—"and *alive* unto God through our Lord Jesus Christ."[8] Our union with Christ in His death and resurrection renders us dead to the old law and alive to the new, emancipating law of the Spirit. The moment of appropriation becomes the moment of realization.

This emancipation from the power of sin is not a gradual process. On one occasion Canon W. Hay Aitken had been preaching a strong sermon on the possibilities of deliverance from the power of sin. As he came out of the church, a young Christian was introduced to him, and they fell into conversation.

"Mr. Aitken, if I could only believe that that was God's method," he said, "I should endeavour to stir my faith to the acceptance of it, but I cannot see that it is God's truth."

"Well, what do you think is God's truth?"

"It seems to me that God's way is to gradually deliver us from our sins. In the process of our experience we shall still have to deplore many falls, many shortcomings, many defeats; but we must go on praying and trying, doing our level best and endeavouring to ask God to assist us. Then we may entertain the hope that, sooner or later, we shall gradually expel bad habits, our falls will be less frequent, our sins not so numerous, and ultimately we shall prove victorious."

Mr. Aitken paused a moment and then said, "Is that your theory about picking pockets?"

"About what?" said he.

"About picking pockets. A pickpocket is converted to God in a London mission. Do you expect that, after a week's experience, on the following Saturday night he will kneel down by his bedside and say: 'O God, I thank Thee for the great and glorious change that has taken place in my life. Last week I stole no less than twenty watches and a couple of dozen purses. This week I have stolen only half a dozen'?"

The young Christian looked rather confused, and Mr. Aitken said, "No, my friend, what you expect is, 'Let him that stole, steal no more'. You expect God to find grace for the thief to enable him to rise above his besetting sin; but if so, why don't you expect God to find grace for you, who are equally redeemed from all iniquity, to rise above your besetting sin, whatever it may be? If you do not expect the thief to go on relapsing into dishonesty, why expect that you yourself are to go on falling and relapsing into your besetting sin?"

This does not mean that relapse into sin becomes impossible, or that sin is eradicated from the nature, but it does mean that bondage to besetting sin is no longer inevitable and inescapable. The law of the Spirit sets free from the law of sin and death.

Sanctification—conformed to His Image.

"God hath from the beginning chosen you to salvation through sanctification of the Spirit and belief of the truth."[9] "Sanctified by the Holy Spirit."[10] These Scriptures indicate that the Holy Spirit plays a dominant part in sanctification, in making the believer holy and like Christ.

"Sanctification is an immediate work of the Spirit of God in the soul of the believer," writes John Owen in a meaty definition, "purifying and cleansing his nature from the pollution and uncleanness of sin, renewing him in the image of God, and thereby enabling him from a spiritual and habitual principle of grace, to yield obedience to God according to the tenor and terms of the New Covenant, by virtue of the life and death of Christ."

Like all other blessings, sanctification may be rightly attributed to all Three Persons of the Trinity. It originates in the purpose of the *Father*.[11] The *Son* is also involved, since it is only through our vital union with Him that the Father's purpose can be achieved.[12] Indeed, He *is* our sanctification.[13] But it is preeminently the work of the *Spirit* Who had been termed the Executive of the Godhead. It is through His effective working that what the Father purposed and the Son made possible, becomes actual in the life of the Christian.[14]

Failure to discriminate between the different senses in which the word "sanctification" is used in the Scriptures, has caused considerable confusion and disappointment.

In one sense of the word, sanctification is *instantaneous and complete*. "By the which will we *have been sanctified* through the offering of the body of Jesus Christ once for all."[15] Here the word refers to that work of Christ *for* the believer which sets him apart to God. It is used in a positional rather than in a moral and experimental sense, and indicates that, upon believing, the Christian is "in Christ" Who is our sanctification.

All believers, irrespective of their spiritual condition are thus set apart to God by the Spirit and participate in this aspect of sanctification. Only in this sense can we understand how Paul could address all the Corinthian believers whom he was rebuking for their gross sin, as "sanctified in Christ Jesus".[16] As to their position they were set apart to God, but they knew little of sanctification as an inward experience of growing conformity to Christ.

But other passages teach that sanctification is *a progressive experience*. "For by one offering He hath perfected for ever them that *are being sanctified*."[17] Operating through the Word of God, in response to faith the Holy Spirit, working *in* the believer, changes him increasingly into the likeness of Christ.

"And all of us . . . are being transformed into the same likeness, from one degree of radiant holiness unto another, even as derived from the Lord the Spirit."[18] This progressive transformation is neither automatic nor inevitable. It is not the natural result of mere effluxion of time. It is tragic though true that many Christians are less Christ-like in old age than they were in their youth. There are degrees of sanctification in this sense of the word. One may be more sanctified than another, who is yet truly sanctified.

While such an experience of progressive sanctification is gloriously possible and is open to every member of the body of Christ, there is no Scriptural warrant for believing that the sinful principle in the heart is eradicated through the refining fires of the Holy Spirit, when all is laid on the altar of sacrifice. "If we say we have no sin, we deceive ourselves."[19]

"I have not sinned for some time," said a woman to Mr. Spurgeon.

"You must be very proud of it," he replied.

"Yes, indeed I am," she rejoined.

The more fully a person is sanctified, the more holy he becomes, the more will he shrink from claiming the attainment of perfect holiness. Even the great Apostle Paul disclaimed any such thing. "Not as though I had already attained, either were already perfect; but I follow after."[20]

He could claim with a clear conscience, "I know nothing against myself," but conscious of the great disparity between his conception of holiness and God's, he hastened to add, "yet am I not hereby justfied."[21] It is the truest holiness of which the possessor is the least conscious.

> *"Spirit of holiness, do Thou*
> *Dwell in this soul of mine;*
> *Possess my heart and make me know*
> *A sanctity Divine."*

REFERENCES

1. John 3:3. 2. Eph. 2:1 RV. 3. John 3:6. 4. 2 Cor. 5:17. 5. 2 Pet. 1:4. 6. John 3:36. 7. 1 Pet. 1:23. 8. Rom. 6:11. 9. 2 Thess. 2:13. 10. Rom. 15:16. 11. Jude 1, 1 Thess. 4:3. 12. Heb. 13:12. 13. 1 Cor. 1:30. 14. 1 Pet. 1:2. 15. Heb. 10:10 RV. 16. 1 Cor. 1:2. 17. Heb. 10:14 RV. 18. 2 Cor. 3:18 Weymouth. 19. 1 John 1:8. 20. Phil. 3:12. 21. 1 Cor. 4:4.

Chapter Eight

THE BAPTISM OF THE SPIRIT

"What then about the now widely current doctrine, that multitudes of Christians have never received the Baptism of the Spirit, and that all such should seek it until they experience it? All I can say is, that such teaching is not derived from the New Testament, and the spread of it is bringing large numbers into bondage and darkness. This error is due, perhaps, to the confusing of the Fulness of the Spirit with the Baptism; but more especially is it due, I think, to a desire to associate with one another the blessing of the Spirit with the gift of Tongues."

W. GRAHAM SCROGGIE

"What this meant was that suddenly and powerfully, to the accompaniment of a sound like wind and a vision of tongues of fire, the Spirit began to overwhelm them with a clear and vivid realization of the glory of their glorified Saviour, to intoxicate them with a thrilling sense of His love and power towards them, and to make it impossible for them to keep quiet; they had to talk about Jesus. Inhibitions were gone; spontaneously, that which filled their hearts overflowed into speech . . . Though the disciples were regenerate and they had known something of the Spirit's ministry prior to Pentecost, this was their first introduction to the full and characteristic experience of new covenant Christianity. As such it was in truth their 'baptism' (the image is essentially initiatory) in the Holy Spirit. The water baptism of John initiated penitents into the expectant community of those who were awaiting the coming of the Messiah; but the Spirit baptism of Christ initiated believers into the life of glory, the experience of realized fellowship with the Messiah who had come, died, risen, and was now at the right hand of God."

J. I. PACKER

THE BAPTISM OF THE SPIRIT

"He shall baptize you with the Holy Spirit."

Matt. 3:11

"Ye shall be baptized with the Holy Spirit not many days hence."

Acts 1:5

"There is one ... baptism."

Eph. 4:5

"By one Spirit were we all baptized into the one body."

1 Cor. 12:13

Considerable divergence of opinion surrounds this subject, with spiritual giants ranged on either side. It is well therefore, to approach our study in humility of mind and with the greatest charity towards those who may not embrace the view that is here espoused.

Here are some conflicting viewpoints:

"The believer may ask and expect a baptism of the Spirit."

ANDREW MURRAY

"The baptism is not, like the filling, presented to us as a blessing for which the Christian is to seek."

BISHOP MOULE

"It does not follow that every believer has received this baptism of the Spirit."

A. J. GORDON

"It is not right that the Christian should profess to be waiting for the baptism of the Spirit."

G. CAMPBELL MORGAN

"Beware of seeking less than the baptism of the Holy Spirit."

HORATIUS BONAR

These representative statements from responsible Bible students whose scholarship and spirituality are beyond question, indicate the two main views on the subject. It is for us to seek the Spirit's enlightenment as we endeavour to arrive at our own conviction on the subject.

Two Variant views

The first view is that the baptism of (or in) the Spirit is *an operation of the Spirit distinct from and additional to His regenerating work, which is to be sought and obtained by the believer.*

The second view is that the baptism of the Spirit is *an event synchronous with the reception of Christ which is never repeated, and need not be sought.*

Before considering these views in detail, we should be clear as to the significance of the phrase "baptism of the Spirit". In the seven references to the phrase, it is each time rendered in the KJV, "baptism *with* the Holy Spirit". More correctly the Greek preposition "en" should be translated *in,* and thus the phrase would be "baptism *in* the Spirit". Throughout this chapter this term will be used, or merely "the baptism". Concerning the preposition *en,* Carr writes: "This preposition is used in Greek to signify the instrument, but it also expresses the surrounding influence or element in which an act takes place."

Subsequent to Regeneration

The view that the baptism is subsequent to regeneration is held by many others than members of Pentecostal churches, but it is a central doctrine of the latter, and is held by most Neo-Pentecostals (as they have come to be called), who remain in the main-line denominational churches. The contention is that though one may be regenerated without this Spirit-baptism, one without this experience is not fully sanctified and does not enjoy full power for service.

It is maintained that the terms "baptized", "filled", "received", "gift", "endued" are all used to describe one and the same experience and are therefore practically synonymous.

The baptism, it is said, is a definite, conscious experience and one may know whether or not he has received it. Such Scriptures as Luke 24:49, Acts 8:15, 16; 19:2 R.V. support this contention. To the question in the last passage, "Did ye receive the Holy Spirit when ye believed?" they were able to answer with a decisive, "No". The experience of the Galatians[1] was so definite and conscious that Paul could appeal to it as a ground for argument.

Further, it is held to be an operation of the Spirit distinct from and additional to His regenerating work. The promise "Ye shall be baptized with the Spirit not many days hence",[2] was given to men already regenerated. Regeneration imparts life, but with the baptism power for service is imparted. However, there may be cases in which the baptism *may* take place at regeneration, e.g. Cornelius.[3] Since it was made possible by the mediatorial work of Christ, it is the birthright of every Christian and awaits his appropriation.

While it is true that every believer *has* the Spirit,[4] it does not of necessity follow that he has experienced the baptism of the Spirit. While every believer has the baptism *potentially*, for the majority it has never become a matter of actual experience, through failure to appropriate it.

The baptism is always connected with testimony and service, and has to do with gifts for service rather than with graces of character.[5] The results will not be the same in each person, since it is the Spirit Who decides how the baptism will be manifested.[6]

The conditions on which this baptism is received are set out by R. M. Riggs, a recognized contemporary Pentecostal writer: (1) We must first be saved; (2) we must obey—that is we must be perfectly surrendered to God; (3) we must ask; (4) we must believe. It is proper to wait or tarry before the Lord to receive this blessing. Such is the first view.

Synchronous with Regeneration

Adherents of this view maintain that the baptism in the Spirit is connected only with the events which centre in and circle around Pentecost. A problem is created by our Lord's promise, "Ye shall be baptized with the Holy Spirit not many days hence,"[7] in that when the promise was fulfilled, no mention is made of the baptism at all. The statement is "they were all filled with the Holy Spirit". For this reason it is contended by those who hold the previous view that the words *baptized* and *filled* may be used interchangeably. But this is by no means necessarily so. The Holy Spirit is not haphazard in His terminology. The whole of our system of interpretation falls to the ground if the words used by the Holy Spirit can be treated in this cavalier fashion.

While both words have reference to the same event and experience, each has its own signification. We might with equal reason say that the words justification and regeneration may be used interchangeably because they refer to the one event and the same moment of time.

Baptism and Filling

The distinction between these words is of vital importance, for much hinges on it. Actually the words "baptism" and "filling", far from being synonymous, are opposite in meaning. By the baptism we are put into the element. By the filling the element is put into us. By the baptism, we are in the Spirit. By the filling, the Spirit is in us. This Spirit-baptism, as in water baptism, is initial, and so far as clear Scripture statement is concerned, is never repeated. On the other hand, the filling may be repeated, or may never be experienced.

The baptism is the *historical event*. The filling is the *human experience*. On the day of Pentecost, both took place simultaneously. Ideally, the same can be, and sometimes is true today, and the believer may be filled with the Spirit from the moment of conversion. But though the ideal, this is far from being the actual. Either through ignorance of the truth or a failure in appropriaton, the filling of the Spirit is often experienced some time after conversion.

Prophetical, Doctrinal, Historical

There are only seven Scriptures which deal specifically with this baptism. Dr. W. Graham Scroggie groups them as follows:

1. Those in which the baptism is viewed *prophetically* as being yet *in prospect*. These are Matt. 3:11; Mark 1:8; Luke 3:16; John 1:33; Acts 1:5. Each of these passages has a future point of time in view. The prediction in these passages applied immediately to the apostles, for it was limited to a point of time, "not many days hence". A historical event was in view. To refer these passages to the experience of believers today would be to put them back before the cross, and make Pentecost a constant necessity, an oft-repeated event.

2. Those in which the baptism is viewed *doctrinally, in retrospect*. The sole reference to the baptism in the Epistles, is 1 Cor. 12:13.

3. Those in which the baptism is viewed *historically*, in *present fulfilment*. Acts 2:1-4; 11:15-17. It was historically necessary, to give a factual basis to our faith.

The prophetical passages point forward. To what? The doctrinal passage points backward. To what? The answer clearly is, to the historical events on the day of Pentecost. It should be noted that Peter identifies Pentecost and the experience in Cornelius' house, with the fulfilment of the Lord's promise of the baptism in the Spirit.[8]

Baptized into the Body of Christ

Since the only passage in the Epistles that deals with our subject is 1 Cor. 12:13, this verse demands careful scrutiny. It is the only verse which sheds clear light on the meaning and purpose of this ministry of the Spirit.

One important result of the baptism in the Spirit is that a union is effected of believers to the body of Christ, which is the Church. Hence we can say that the baptism is the work of the Holy Spirit in forming and adding to the Church.

It should be remembered that the Book of Acts is an incomplete stage of revelation. It is a record of "all that Jesus *began* both to do and teach",[9] a record of the continued activity of the ascended Christ as He gave shape to His Church and its doctrine. But the experiences of the apostles in founding the Church are not necessarily the norm for today. In point of fact, none of the experiences in connection with the baptism in the Spirit recorded in the Acts, even those in the house of Cornelius, can be exactly duplicated today. Hence the importance of the verse we are studying.

From this text four facts emerge:

1. This baptism is *common to all* believers, and not the experience of a select few. The tense is *"were* we *all* baptized". (RV). This "all" included some who had even been guilty of immorality and eating food sacrificed to idols.

2. It is *a past event* in the believer's life. The aorist tense indicates this, *"were* we all".

3. It refers to the believer being *incorporated into the body of Christ* by a vital, organic union effected by the Holy Spirit. Through this union he is "in Christ" with all the resultant benefits and blessings.

4. There is *no distinction among believers* in this respect. The baptism assures the unity of the members who constitute the body. "By one Spirit were ye all baptized into one body, whether we be Jews or Gentiles"—all privilege had come to an end; "whether we be bond or free"—all disability had ceased, through participation in this Spirit baptism, "and have been all made to drink into one Spirit".

Some claim that while the first clause refers to the salvation experience of believers, the last clause of this verse refers to the baptism in the Spirit in the Pentecostal sense and that therefore the verse speaks of two experiences, salvation and Spirit-baptism. The second clause, however, is parallel to the first in stressing the oneness of believers, and by the use of "all", indicates that it applies to all believers. Any other interpretation destroys Paul's argument.

As it was then, so is it today. Scripture nowhere exhorts believers to seek this baptism, nor is there any distinction made between those who have and those who have not been so baptized. It is presented as a fact common to all believers. The experience to be sought is not the baptism, but the filling.

Three Special Groups

This interpretation of 1 Cor. 12:13 would appear to be supported by the fact that it affords a satisfying explanation of the three instances of the baptism recorded in the book of Acts, a subject which is more fully treated later.

At Pentecost the Spirit was poured out only upon the *Jewish believers* who had assembled from far and near. While they themselves were looking for this promised effusion, the idea that it would be enjoyed by others than Jews never occurred to them.

The next group were the *Gentiles* who were the objects of Jewish contempt. It required a thrice-repeated command from heaven to overcome Peter's Jewish exclusiveness.[10] The thought of Gentiles being incorporated into the Church on an equality with Jews was too revolutionary for him. God therefore sovereignly intervened to achieve His purpose. Without the laying on of hands, and while Peter was in the midst of his sermon in the home of Cornelius, God interrupted and bestowed on the Gentiles the identical gift of the Spirit to that poured out at Pentecost.[11]

A third isolated religious group were *the disciples of John Baptist,* many of whom apparently knew only John's baptism of repentance. They too must be incorporated into the Christian Church through the baptism in the Spirit, and this took place through Paul's instrumentality.[12]

The Contemporary Parallel

It will be noted that each of these incidents is concerned with a unique religious group, and *not one of them exactly parallels the case of the believer today.* Hence the wisdom of taking our teaching on this subject from the apostle's teaching rather than by endeavouring to imitate the experience of one group or another.

The experience which would be the norm for the believer today would be that of the apostle's converts, who received Christ as we do, *after* the Holy Spirit was given. The fact that the apostles lived before Christ's baptism, during His earthly ministry and after His ascension, necessarily places them in a class by themselves.

Is Tarrying Necessary?

That the one hundred and twenty disciples did tarry in the upper room in Jerusalem is an indisputable fact. They were commanded to do so by their Lord.[13] They tarried in the specific location assigned, Jerusalem, the reason being that in that location God planned to bestow the promised gift of the Holy Spirit. They obeyed, and He fulfilled His promise. There is no implication in this historic event that this has a spiritual counterpart in the experience of the Christian today, for the command could be obeyed and the promise fulfilled in no other place than Jerusalem.

The key to the problem hinges on whether or not the tarrying of the believers *caused* the descent of the Spirit. The answer would seem to be in the negative. The Spirit descended "when the day of Pentecost was finally come",[14] after the risen Son had been glorified,[15] when the day preordained by God for this momentous event had arrived.

The Holy Spirit, as has been pointed out earlier, could have come on no other day than that on which He came, the day of Pentecost, foreshadowed in Leviticus 23, any more than Christ could have been crucified on any other than the Passover feast day. The obedience of the disciples put them in the place and condition where they could be recipients of the blessings attendant on the Gift, but their tarrying was in no way the securing means of the Pentecostal effusion. The Gift was dependent on the sovereign will of God, not on the subjective condition of the recipients.

Bishop Moule makes this comment: "May I say with tenderness and deep spiritual sympathy that a mistake seems to underlie the practice not uncommon now among earnest Christians, of 'waiting' for a special baptism of the Spirit in order to more effectual service for the Lord. Surely 'by one Spirit *we have been* baptized into one body'. And now our part is to open in humblest faith all the avenues and regions of the soul, that we might be filled with what we already have."

Any cause of waiting for the fulness of the Holy Spirit is on our side, not on God's. He can do no more than He has done.

Summary

The following appear valid reasons for non-acceptance of the view that the baptism in the Spirit is an operation distinct from and additional or subsequent to His regenerating work, which is to be sought and obtained by the believer.

1. To say that the words "baptized", "filled" or "received" can be used interchangeably and are practically synonymous, is a gratuitous assumption which lacks support both in Scripture and etymology.

2. This view appears to confuse the historic event with the human experience.

3. This view is based on the insupportable assumption that our experience today is on all fours with that of the apostles and others at Pentecost.

4. The power for service received by the disciples on the day of Pentecost is said to be the result of the filling, not of the baptism.[16]

5. This view has no satisfactory exegetical explanation of the significance of 1 Cor. 12:13, the only verse in the Epistles bearing clearly on the subject.

6. It tends to make the happenings on the day of Pentecost dependent on the subjective condition of the apostles rather than on the sovereign will of God.

7. There is no command to be baptized in the Spirit, nor is there Scriptural support for the view that some Christians are so baptized while others are not.

8. The same experience contended for unscripturally we believe, in this view, is Scripturally provided for in the view that the baptism in the Spirit is a historic and never repeated event contemporaneous with the reception of Christ, which was at Pentecost accompanied by the filling of the Spirit. The blessed human experience sprang from the filling, not the baptism of the Spirit.

REFERENCES

1. Gal. 3:2. 2. Acts 1:5. 3. Acts 10:45. 4. Rom. 8:9. 5. Luke 24:49, Acts 1:8. 6. 1 Cor. 12:4–13. 7. Acts 1:5. 8. Acts 11:15–17. 9. Acts 1:1. 10. Acts 10:16. 11. Acts 11:15. 12. Acts 19:1–7. 13. Luke 24:49. 14. Acts 2:1. 15. John 7:39. 16. Acts 2:4.

Chapter Nine

THE REVEALER OF CHRIST

" 'He shall bear witness of Me.' This reliance of Jesus on the Holy Spirit has suffered no disappointment. As the second Christian millennium now verges towards its close, the largeness, the amplitude, of what has been done overtaxes the imagination. A fragmentary rehearsal of it, a mere skeleton, shows that in His witness-bearing the Holy Spirit has wrought worthily of Himself and worthily of Him on Whom He fixes attention. With viewless operation, and with complete self-effacement, He has been engrossed in the trust committed to Him."

JOHN MCNAUGHER

"It was the delight of the Son to glorify the Father; it is the delight of the Spirit to glorify the Son. Not that the Holy Spirit adds anything to the personal and mediatorial glories which now encircle Him as seàted on the throne of His glory; but the Holy Spirit glorifies Jesus *in the view and experience of men.* Indeed, it is truly delightful to notice the different instances of glorifying that we have here. The Son glorified the Father *on earth*; the Father glorified the Son *in heaven*; and now again the Holy Spirit glorifies Christ *on the earth*, in the hearts of His people."

CHARLES ROSS

THE REVEALER OF CHRIST

"He shall glorify me . . ."

John 16:14

"He shall receive of mine and show it unto you. He shall testify of me."

John 15:26

The ministry of the Spirit is Christo-centric. The test of any professed movement of the Spirit whether in personal or corporate experience is the place it gives to Christ. If it glorifies man or magnifies some spiritual experience, it lacks the hallmark of the Spirit.

The function of the telescope is not to reveal itself, but the glories it brings into the range of vision. The ministry of the Holy Spirit is to conceal Himself behind the scenes, and give prominence to Jesus Christ. So self-effacing has He been in the discharge of His trust, that His own very existence has been questioned. Any knowledge we have of Christ has been imparted through the Spirit's illumination of the Scriptures He has inspired. As the Spirit of Christ, He delights to unveil His glories to believing hearts.

There is no rivalry within the unity of the Godhead, for in Scripture each Person is represented as delighting to serve the Other. Christ's passion was to glorify, to manifest the hidden excellence of the Father. "I seek not my own glory", He affirmed. "If I glorify myself, my glory is nothing."[1] His work had reached its zenith when He claimed, "I have glorified Thee on the earth".[2]

The author of the letter to the Hebrews advances the fact that "Christ glorified not Himself",[3] as one of His qualifications for priesthood. Jesus also gave glory to the Spirit. Did He not assure His disciples that it was expedient for them that He should go away, or else the Comforter would not come? In this way He implied that the Holy Spirit would more than compensate for His physical absence.

In His High-priestly prayer, the Son's petition was, "Father, the hour is come, glorify Thy Son. . . . And now O Father, glorify me with Thyself."[4] This the Father did when He raised Him from the dead and received Him into glory, saying, "Sit Thou at my right hand until I make Thine enemies Thy footstool." Thus the Father glorifies the Son.

The Lover of Christ

The Spirit in turn is jealous for the glory of the Son. In speaking of those who had adulterously turned away from Christ to other loves, the apostle James wrote, "Do ye think that the Scripture saith in vain, the Spirit that dwelleth in us yearneth for us even unto jealous envy?"[5] He cannot bear to see a cooling of love for Christ. He longs to see the Lamb of God vindicated and adored in the scene of His humiliation and rejection. To this end He directs all His powers.

The Spirit's primary concern is to glorify Christ, and to secure the acknowledgment and practical manifestation of His Lordship in our lives. He does not add anything to the personal glories of the ascended Christ, but He glorifies Him in the experience of men. He reveals and explains Him. You cannot see a person in a dark room; You may even be ignorant of his presence. But let someone switch on the light and the person stands revealed. "What light is to the earth, the Holy Spirit is to Christ", said Joseph Parker.

The glory of the exalted Christ staggers the imagination. When John the aged who had leaned on His bosom, had gazed on the outshining of His majesty on the Transfiguration Mount, was confronted with the vision of his exalted Lord, he "fell at his feet as dead".[6] The Spirit delights to give glimpses of Christ's transcendent glory.

The Veil Removed

"The veil is upon their heart," was Paul's diagnosis of the spiritual blindness of Israel. A veil so thick that even the blaze of Christ's divine glory could not penetrate it, lies between the human soul and Christ. Only by the operation of the Spirit can that veil be removed and Christ savingly revealed. When He lived on earth as man, many saw, heard and touched Him who were not transformed by the experience. And why? Because they would not permit the Spirit to lift the veil and illumine to them the face of Jesus Christ, their Messiah. They knew Him after the flesh, but not after the Spirit.

The first activity of the Holy Spirit after He had been bestowed on the infant Church on the day of Pentecost, was to bear witness to the exalted Christ to Jews assembled "out of every nation under heaven".[7] The human instrument He used was a horny-handed fisherman. He mastered Peter's personality and powers with amazing effect. What persuasive eloquence! What skilful exegesis! What burning logic! What unction!

The whole impromptu sermon was a powerful presentation of the risen and exalted Christ to those who had crucified Him. Ancient prophecies, long dormant in his mind, flashed with new meaning, and under the Spirit's anointing, were seen to apply to the Saviour.[8]

Acting for the first time under His new commission, the Holy Spirit, through Peter, with master strokes portrayed on the canvas the face of Jesus Christ. Through His convicting power, the assembled multitudes, among whom were many who had cried "Crucify Him!", were pricked to the heart. Before nightfall three thousand had become His disciples—a fitting inauguration of the Holy Spirit into His role of "Revealer of Christ".

Christ in the Scriptures

"He shall receive of mine and shall show it unto you",[9] said the Master. He will receive the unsearchable riches of Christ Who claimed, "All things that the Father hath are mine"—in order to show them to His people—riches of divine glory, divine merit, divine grace.

The medium used by the Spirit for this revelation of the things of Christ, is the *external revelation* of Him recorded in the Spirit-inspired Word. In it, "Holy men of God spoke as they were moved by the Holy Spirit."[10] It is pre-eminently in the Scriptures that the Spirit shows to us the things of Christ. It is true that "the letter killeth",[11] but under the illumination and interpretation of the Divine Author, the words become spirit and life.

To the anointed eye the Old Testament becomes full of Christ. Every page reveals some new facet of His Person and work. In the Levitical sacrificial system His mediatorial and expiatory work are foreshadowed. The Tabernacle is a pictorial representation to Israel of the glories and ministry of the coming Messiah. In the Prophets His greatness and achievements, as well as His sufferings and glory, are anticipated. The Spirit-taught believer can again experience the burning heart kindled in the Emmaus disciples when Jesus, "beginning at Moses and all the prophets, expounded unto them *in all the scriptures* the things concerning Himself".[12]

There is no joy comparable to that of seeing the light of heaven breaking on the face of one to whom for the first time,

Christ has been revealed. Every soul-winner can recall instances in which the inquirer has been clearly and cogently shown the way of salvation, but despite all explanation and illustration, he remains in complete spiritual darkness. The Scriptures which seem so clear and unmistakable to the counsellor, are to him an impenetrable mystery.

At last, at the end of his resources and in complete dependence on the Holy Spirit, the counsellor has gone over the ground once again and suddenly, without human explanation, the troubled countenance has cleared, and the inquirer exclaims, "I see it all now, why did I not see it before?" What caused the change? Not a clearer presentation of the truth, but to the now surrendered will, the Spirit has been able to tear away the veil and reveal the Saviour.

In describing a wonderful meeting in which a number of alcoholics had been born anew, the preacher said, "I simply held up Jesus Christ, and it pleased the Holy Spirit to illumine His face, and men saw and believed". That was model preaching.

Christ in the Heart

The Spirit is not content with a mere exterior revelation of Christ. In referring to the Spirit's power at work in the Church and in the hearts of Christians, A. W. Tozer wrote, "This power can go straight to its object with piercing directness; it can diffuse itself through the mind like an infinitely volatile essence securing ends above and beyond the limits of the intellect. It does not create objects that are not there, but reveals objects already present and hidden from the soul. In actual human experience this is likely to be first felt in *a heightened sense of the presence of Christ*. He is felt to be a real Person and to be intimately, ravishingly near."

Christ was revealed *to* Paul on the Damascus road, to the accompaniment of "a light above the brightness of the noonday sun".[13] As a result of this transforming vision, the Christ Who had been the object of his implacable hatred, became the object of his adoring worship.

But this experience, cataclysmic though it was, is not the full explanation of Paul's flaming ministry. This exterior vision of Christ was followed by an equally transfiguring revelation of Christ *within his heart*.[14] From that moment there was a new dimension in Paul's experience. "I no longer live ... Christ liveth in me."[15] "To me to live is Christ."[16]

75

"It is my confident belief", said Dr. F. B. Meyer when addressing a large congregation, "that there is not a single man or woman who believes in Christ who has not Christ in the heart. But remember, that as a heavy veil hid the holy of holies from the holy place, so Jesus Christ may be in your heart; but because you have never realized He is there, because you have made no use of His presence there, because you have been unbelieving and may be indolent to respond to His appeal, though He has been in your heart ever since you were regenerate, His presence has been hidden from your eyes; it has been veiled. I pray God that the two hands that rent the veil of the temple from the top to the bottom, may rend the veil in your inner life, that the Christ Who is there may be revealed in you."

Christ Formed Within

The Holy Spirit does not rest content with even such a wonderful revelation as this. His passion for glorifying Christ is such that He desires every believing heart to be "conformed to His image". With this objective in view He patiently works, "until Christ be formed in you".[17]

When an egg is laid, amid the fluid there floats a tiny speck of life. As the egg is incubated the embryo gradually increases while the fluid diminishes. At the end of three weeks, no trace of fluid is left. The fully-formed chick pecks its way out of the confining shell and embarks on life in a new world.

When the new life enters the believing heart, it is an embryo life. It must be nurtured on "the sincere milk of the Word".[18] Through periods of devout meditation on the Scriptures and seasons of waiting on God, the Holy Spirit fosters and develops that life from within, until the likeness of Christ is more and more apparent without.

> "Spirit of Jesus, glorify
> The Master's name in me;
> Whether I live, or if I die,
> Let Christ exalted be."

REFERENCES

1. John 8:54. 2. John 17:4, 5. 3. Heb. 5:4. 4. Heb. 10:13. 5. Jas. 4:5. 6. Rev. 1:17. 7. Acts 2:5. 8. Acts 2:16. 9. John 16:14. 10. 2 Pet. 1:21. 11. 2 Cor. 3:6. 12. Luke 24:27. 13. Acts 26:13. 14. Gal. 1:16. 15. Gal. 2:20. 16. Phil. 1:21. 17. Gal. 1:19. 18. 1 Pet. 2:2.

Chapter Ten

THE ADMINISTRATOR OF
THE CHURCH

"The Holy Ghost from the day of Pentecost has occupied an entirely new position. The whole administration of the affairs of the Church of Christ has since that day devolved upon Him . . . That day was the installation of the Holy Spirit as the Administrator of the Church in all things, which office He is to exercise according to circumstances at His discretion. It is as vested with such authority that He gives His name to this dispensation . . . There is but one other great event to which Scripture directs us to look, and that is the second coming of the Lord. Till then we live in the Pentecostal age and under the rule of the Holy Ghost."

J. ELDER CUMMING

"When Christ ascended to the Father He sent forth the Spirit who should be His Vicegerent in the Church; and as long as the Sovereign reigns in heaven, His spiritual Viceroy reigns in human souls. They are correspondent and correlative the one to the other. 'If I go not away', said the Saviour before He ascended, the 'Spirit cannot come'. If He be away, then the Spirit is in the Church; the absence of one is the presence of the other; or let me rather say that there is no absence, no distance, no departure, no separation! Christ Himself is one with His Holy Spirit, and with Him templed in the heart of His mystical body."

ARCHER BUTLER

THE ADMINISTRATOR OF THE CHURCH

*"Take heed to all the flock over which the Holy Spirit
hath made you overseers, to feed the Church of God."*

Acts 20:28

The Holy Spirit is sovereignly responsible for all that pertains
to the life and administration of the Church. He it was Who
brought it into being, and on Him devolves its effective functioning. Prior to the day of Pentecost the disciples were a band of
individuals, but the fiery baptism fused them into one corporate
whole, "the Church which is His body".[1] It is an organism
as the metaphor of the body implies, not a mere organization,
"For by one baptism were we all baptized into one body". It
comprises all those who throughout the world are in living
union with Christ the Head.

In the incarnation, a physical body was prepared for the
Son of God, in which He could identify Himself with men and
achieve their salvation. There was no such incarnation for the
Holy Spirit, but His vehicle of expression and ministry is the
mystical body of Christ. It has been said that the body prepared
for the Eternal Son was begotten of the Holy Spirit and born of
a virgin; the body for the indwelling Spirit is begotten of faith in
Jesus Christ, the Son of the living God.

The Vicar of Christ, as the Holy Spirit has been called, earnestly desires to administer His beneficent yet holy rule in the
Church, but unfortunately in our day the will of the majority
has almost entirely displaced the will of the Spirit. The
members of the Body are more and more usurping the prerogatives of the Spirit. This usurpation of His office and functions
is in large measure responsible for the Laodicean condition of
many churches. But once allow Him His rightful position, however, and churches will begin to throb with new spiritual life.

Recognition of His Office

Perhaps an example of the way in which the Spirit responded
to a recognition of His place and administration in the Church
will illuminate this truth.

Dr. A. T. Pierson told of a young vicar in England who found

78

himself in charge of a parish that had extreme ritualistic practices, and with them secular tendencies equally pronounced. The spirit of prayer and the Spirit of God had little recognition or administrative control.

The congregation was large and outward signs of prosperity abundant, but the new vicar felt it was all a deceptive facade and that there was little true spiritual life in the church. With much prayer he began to preach against compromise with the world and adoption of worldly schemes, and insisted on a Scriptural, prayerful, and spiritual walk and service.

The church began to empty. So rapid was the decline in the congregation that a deputation of twelve men representing the officers and others went to the bishop to protest against the vicar's methods. The bishop sent his wife, a gifted woman, to visit the parish and especially the vicar.

She was kindly received, and enquired his reasons for the course he was pursuing in demolishing the work as he found it in the parish. He frankly showed how far the former ways were from Scripture. Then, kneeling with the bishop's wife he earnestly sought light from above. In the midst of his praying, the bishop's wife said, "Pray no longer. You are right and I am wrong."

The vicar went on with his reforms until there were few left to reform. One morning he found only two persons present. They were in sympathy, however, and in place of the usual service, they spent an hour and a half in prayer. They pleaded with God to take off them the burden of responsibility, and Himself take charge of the Church.

A powerful work of the Spirit at once began, The firstfruits were the twelve men who had waited on the bishop to have the vicar removed. All were converted. The church filled up with a new congregation in part, and in part with a transformed body of people, who formerly were entirely worldly in spirit.

Prayer became a prevailing habit. The Holy Spirit was recognized as the presiding Officer in all church life. The gospel was preached simply, and God's blessing conspicuously rested on all the work.

Later, the bishop himself visited the parish. He inquired of one of the church wardens who was a mechanic the number of communicants.

"We never count the communicants," he replied, "but when the Lord's Supper is celebrated, few, if any go out, and the church is always full."

"But," said the bishop, "how do you keep your communicants

together seeing you have no guilds and societies and festivals?"

"Well, I'll tell you," replied the simple working man. "Our vicar first gets his people soundly converted, then he gets them filled with the Holy Spirit, and then the Holy Spirit keeps them, and we don't have to keep them at all."

Turning to his chaplain, the bishop said, "We have nothing like this in the diocese." This church supported several missionaries, and using New Testament methods, the vicar had more money than was needed.

A prominent Christian whose work involved him in wide travel, as he watched the development of this church, said that he knew of nothing that appeared to so closely resemble and reproduce apostolic times. And it was the result of recognizing and according to the Holy Spirit His rightful place in the church.

Selections of Officers

The appointment of the officers of the Church, from greatest to least, lies primarily not with the membership but with the Holy Spirit. This is the obvious significance of Paul's words: "The Church . . . over which the Holy Spirit hath made you overseers."

Where there is a prayerful waiting on Him for guidance, and a subjection to His will, His selection will be made unmistakably plain. Where the Spirit's presidency and direction is recognized, the attaining of unanimity in matters under discussion becomes a practical possibility. "It seemed good to the Holy Spirit and to us . . .," read the findings of the Church Council at Jerusalem.[2]

It is instructive to note that the man chosen to fill the place on the apostolate vacated by Judas passes into obscurity. Was it because Christ had not yet sent the Holy Spirit as Administrator of the Church, and that it was not the prerogative of the apostles to choose, but His right to give "to some, apostles"?[3] Two years later He exercised His prerogative in selecting Saul of Tarsus.

The Divine plan has not changed. The men who are to administer the affairs of the Church in His name, must be one with Him in aim, and willing to accept His will in everything. Accordingly, even those who are to fill only subordinate and temporal offices must be "men full of the Holy Spirit".[4]

The appointment to church offices of influential or wealthy men who lack spiritual fitness, quenches the working of the

Spirit in the Church, since it ousts Him from His rightful position. A worldly or unregenerate church officer is leaven that will eventually permeate the whole lump. Is it not significant that each of the letters to the Seven Churches[5] closes with: "He that hath an ear, let him hear what the Spirit saith to the churches"? The inference is that not all churches are listening to His voice.

Bestowal of Gifts

More than human qualifications are required for the discharge of an officer's duties in the church. So, in His administration of the Church, one of the Holy Spirit's first activities was to bestow on selected men the gifts necessary for its effective functioning.[6]

Apart from Him there would be no spiritual gifts, and apart from His co-working, no gifts are spiritually effective. Every church in which the Spirit's right to administer is recognized will, in greater or lesser degree be a spiritually gifted church, for His gifts are but the manifestation of the Spirit Himself in His manifold wisdom and working.

As this theme will be more fully treated later we pass on to a consideration of His presidency over the

Ministries of the Church

Our Lord's last words before His ascension, "Ye shall receive power after the Holy Spirit is come upon you and ye shall be witnesses unto me,"[7] indicated that the *witness* of the Church must be in the power of the Spirit. It was this factor which made Paul's witness so mightily effective.[8]

When they became filled with the Spirit, the witness to the resurrection of their Lord of the once fearful and timid disciples became singularly powerful.[9] In his first Letter, Peter revealed the secret of his power on the day of Pentecost—he preached the gospel "with the Holy Spirit sent down from heaven".[10] The secret of all power in preaching lies in being entirely mastered by the Spirit and becoming the channel of His power.

It is this subtle something that constitutes the difference between a true sermon and a speech. Paul recognized this essential difference when he claimed "My speech and my preaching was not with enticing words of man's wisdom, but in demonstration of the Spirit and of power."[11] "Our gospel came unto you not in word only, but also in power and in the Holy Spirit."[12]

The *worship* of the Church is also under his direction. "We are the circumcision," said Paul, "which worship God in the Spirit."[13] *Prayer* is not to be vain repetition. Believers are to pray "in the Holy Spirit".[14] The disciples' petition, "Lord teach us to pray", found its answer in the gift of the Spirit Who would help their infirmities and initiate them into the art of intercession.[15]

Even the *praise and singing* of the Church is to be in the control of the Spirit. "Be filled with the Spirit, speaking to yourselves in psalms and hymns and spiritual songs, singing and making melody in your heart to the Lord."[16] This fact alone should preclude an unregenerate person from being entrusted with responsibility for the ministry of song.

The voice of the Spirit may still be heard in the churches when their leaders take time to let it be heard. "As they"—the leaders—"ministered to the Lord and fasted, the Holy Spirit said...."[17] And again, "He that hath an ear, let him hear what the Spirit saith to the churches."[18]

REFERENCES

1. Eph. 1:23. 2. Acts 15:28. 3. Eph. 4:11. 4. Acts 6:3. 5. Rev. 2 and 3. 6. 1 Cor. 12:8, 28, Eph. 4:11. 7. Acts 1:8, 8. 1 Cor. 2:4. 9. Acts 4:31, 33. 10. 1 Pet. 1:12. 11. 1 Cor. 2:4. 12. 1 Thess. 1:5. 13. Phil. 3:3. 14. Eph. 6:18. 15. Rom. 8:26, 27. 16. Eph. 5:18, 19. 17. Acts 13:2. 18. Rev. 2:7.

Chapter Eleven

THE EXECUTOR OF THE GREAT COMMISSION

"As in the first giving of the Holy Spirit an elect and blood-sprinkled church has been made ready to diffuse Him, so in the final great Pentecost witnessing churches must be planted among all nations to constitute the vessels and receptacles of the Spirit-distributing centres, if we may say so, for the outflow of the Holy Spirit to the yet unsaved millions."

A. J. GORDON

"The history of modern missions, it has been well said, is but a continuation of the Acts of the Apostles. And what is the Acts of the Apostles but the first chapter of the history of the Holy Spirit in the Church? Have not the later chapters of that history been constantly unfolding, and have they not been substantially identical with the first? And would not this identity be apparent if only we had the record of it written by an inspired pen? I verily believe so."

A. J. GORDON

THE EXECUTOR OF THE
GREAT COMMISSION

"Ye shall receive power after that the Holy Ghost is come upon you, and ye shall be witnesses unto me ... unto the uttermost part of the earth."

Acts 1:8

"The Holy Spirit said, 'Separate me Barnabas and Saul for the work whereunto I have called them'."

Acts 13:2

In the great missionary manual of the Church, the book of the Acts of the Apostles, we meet the name of the Holy Spirit on almost every page. He appears as the Executor of the Great Commission and the Administrator of the missionary enterprise. The history related is a sustained narrative of His activity through the Church.

When our Lord broke to His disciples the news of His impending departure, He promised a Viceregent Who would be their Companion and Counsellor.[1] His promise, as we have seen, was fulfilled on the day of Pentecost, when they exchanged His physical presence for His omnipresence in the person of His Spirit. From the moment of the Spirit's advent, He devoted Himself to fulfil the yearning of the Saviour's heart—world-wide evangelism. The promise of power for the disciples was specific, and the fulfilment equally definite. The Spirit came upon them and they witnessed effectively, but in the record of their missionary activity, it is everywhere apparent that the acts of the apostles are traced beyond the human channel to the Divine source. The main Actor is the Holy Spirit, and men are His instruments in achieving the Divine purpose.

The day of Pentecost marked two significant events in the onward march of Christianity. First, *the inauguration of the Holy Spirit* into His twofold Office of Comforter and Enduer. As Comforter, He was imparted to His sorrowing disciples by the Risen Christ when "He breathed on them and said, 'Receive ye the Holy Spirit'."[2] The promise of the Son was of the Holy Spirit as Comforter.

84

The promise of the Father was as Enduer[3] and it found its fulfilment on the day of Pentecost, when "they were all filled with the Holy Spirit".[4] It was this epoch-making event that marked the real beginning of the missionary enterprise.

The inauguration of the Paraclete into His twofold office was accompanied by another epoch-making event, *the institution of the Church,* the mystical Body of Christ. In the days of His flesh, our Lord provided a perfect vehicle for the Holy Spirit to use in fulfilling God's eternal purpose on earth. But with the removal of Christ's physical body, His mystical Body became the instrument of the Spirit. All Christ did on earth was through the empowering of the Spirit, and ideally the same should be true of His Church. The baptism of the Spirit had a corporate significance, for by it all believers were incorporated into the Body of Christ,[5] and this organism, through its members, was charged with the responsibility of world-wide witness.[6]

Enduer of Missionaries

They were to find power for witnessing in the enduement of the Spirit. In His final utterance, the ascending Lord linked the advent of His Spirit with the enduement of power for witness "to the uttermost part of the earth".[7] His words were fulfilled on the day of Pentecost which was a sample of which subsequent missions were to be the facsimile. This enduement is still the essential missionary equipment today, for apart from the Spirit's co-witness, there can be no effective human witness to Christ.

Executor of the Great Commission

At the commencement of the new dispensation, the authority of the Spirit was vindicated by His strange work of judgment in the case of Ananias and Sapphira. The sin of lying to the Holy Spirit brought on both of them the dire penalty of sudden death. "Why hath Satan filled thine heart to lie to the Holy Spirit? . . . Thou hast not lied unto men but unto God."[8] God would impress men with the fact that it is no light thing to trifle with the Holy Spirit Who is His Representative on earth.

His first administrative activity was *the calling of the missionaries.*[9] The initiative in the missionary call is with the Holy Spirit, not with the volunteer or the church. The paragraph recounting the sending out of Barnabas and Saul sheds helpful light on this subject. "Separate me Barnabas and Saul for the work where unto *I have called them,"* was the message of the

Spirit to the leaders of the church at Antioch. The divine call preceded any activity of church or missionary. The responsibility of the church was to let them go, to recognize the Spirit's appointment and act upon it.

It is worthy of note that the Holy Spirit selected the ablest men in the church for His purpose, and, recognizing His right to do so, the church made no demur. The responsibility of the missionary was to respond to the call.

In the final analysis, judgment of fitness lay neither with the individual nor with the church leaders but with the Holy Spirit Who communicated His mind to them. The church did not vote on the issue. The candidates did not submit sheaves of testimonials. The favoured two were discovered to a group of spiritual leaders of the church in which they were serving, while they "ministered to the Lord", in prayer and self denial. It has not always been so. Especially in the early days of modern missions, missionaries went out in the teeth of overwhelming opposition or indifference of a church insensitive to the voice of the Spirit. Mighty men like Ramon Lull and William Carey went out in spite of the church. Though neglected by men, they were not forgotten by the Spirit Who called them.

The Spirit *sent out the missionaries* with the church as consenting and supporting party. "So they, *being sent forth by the Holy Spirit,* departed into Seleucia." The fellowship of the church was symbolized in the laying on of hands, but the authorizing thrust came from the Holy Spirit, the real Consecrator. The church dedicated and commissioned those whom He had already consecrated. Without the prior ordination of the Spirit, the laying on of men's hands is in vain.

The selection of the sphere of work was also the prerogative of the Spirit, not of the church or the missionaries. He alone knows the strategy of the Lord of the harvest Whose interests He serves. Paul's journeys afford striking proof of this.

On their first journey the Spirit guided the missionaries to Cyprus, on the sea route to Asia and the Roman world. Of their second journey we are told, "Now when they had gone throughout Phrygia and the region of Galatia, and were *forbidden of the Holy Spirit* to preach the Word in Asia ... they assayed to go into Bithynia, but *the Spirit suffered them not.*"[10]

The Holy Spirit alone knows which are strategic centres, and who is best fitted to serve there. William Carey planned to go to the South Sea Islands. The Spirit designated him to India— and with what amazing results. Thomas Barnardo felt called to China, but the Spirit retained him in England to bring blessing and salvation to thousands of children. Adoniram Judson's objective was India. The Spirit directed his steps to Burma. In the light of subsequent developments, how important it was that they were sensitive to the Spirit's voice.

It was not that the Spirit had no purpose of grace for Mysia and Bithynia—they were to receive the gospel in due time— but for the present, the divine strategy was that the evangel should be carried westward to Europe, whence would stem the great missionary movement that would encircle the globe. Europe was ripening for harvest. Anglo-Saxons with their lust for travel were to be the missionary pioneers, and in fact, five-sixths of all missionary work has been done through their instrumentality.

Paul was sensitive to the Spirit's restraint, and did not press forward in self-will. Instead, he withdrew to discover in prayer, meditation and consultation, God's will for him and his companions. In passing, it should be noted that the expansion of the church and its extension to unexpected quarters, was due, not to the deliberate planning of the missionaries, but to the constraint of the Spirit.

The Spirit determines *the timing of the missionary programme*. How very slow God appears to be at times! Why wait a dozen and more years from the completion of the events on which Christianity is based before fully launching His world-wide missionary programme? And why send out only two? Why so paltry a task force in the face of such appalling need? We have to learn that God's ways are not our ways and His thoughts are higher than our thoughts. It is for us to heed the Spirit's restraint, and wait on Him for the revelation of His timing. There is such a thing as the tide of the Spirit. He is working to a meticulously accurate timetable, and we disregard His timing to our own loss and disappointment. We can with profit recall Paul's words, "He fixed the epochs of their history."

The appointment of fellow-workers is also in the sphere of the Spirit's authority. Saul did not choose Barnabas as his partner, he was assigned by the Holy Spirit. Even the brilliant and deeply taught apostle was not commissioned to go out without a more experienced and spiritually strong senior. The association of these two was no mere chance happening. Barnabas was mature, experienced, a "son of consolation". To his gracious gifts and personality, the Spirit added the intensity, fiery zeal, restless urgency and brilliant intellectual powers of Saul, who had for some time been experiencing the tempering of his spirit in the school of God. Together they possessed a striking blending of gifts. But even in a team divinely selected and spiritually alert, there later came a rift in the lute over John Mark, Barnabas' nephew, and the two men separated.[11] Even this regrettable incident was over-ruled by the Spirit, so that two preaching bands were created, instead of one.

Another activity of the Holy Spirit is in *leading the missionary to strategic converts*. The outstanding Biblical example of this is the call of the Spirit to Philip, to leave the thriving revival in Samaria in which he was a leading figure, and go "to Gaza which is desert". On the face of it this sounded unreasonable. But when in obedience to the Spirit's voice Philip reached Gaza, his arrival exactly synchronized with that of a vastly important African in search of Christ and His salvation.[12] It was the reward of his unquestioning obedience to be invited to explain the gospel to a prepared seeker who received Christ as Saviour on the spot. Through this convert who was none other than Ethiopia's Chancellor of the Exchequer, the good news penetrated that distant Kingdom. Apart from the Spirit's sovereign intervention, Philip would never have gone to Gaza, and the Ethiopian Eunuch would have remained unenlightened. Every mission field provides similar, if less spectacular examples.

The pressures of the powers of darkness is one of the acute problems of missionary work. At times the conflict seems intolerable, but here, too, the Spirit is active in *empowering against Satanic opposition*. It was not long before the missionaries experienced resistance. Elymas the sorcerer withstood Barnabas and Saul, seeking to turn the deputy Sergius Paulus, away from the faith. The Spirit enabled Saul to cope with his opposition. "Then Saul, *filled with the Holy Spirit* . . . said, O full of all subtlety and mischief . . . wilt thou not cease to pervert the right ways of the Lord? . . . Thou shalt be blind."[13]

Saul experienced through this special filling the cooperation of the Spirit in dealing with Satan-inspired opposition. The Spirit first imparted to him spiritual insight to discern the source of the disturbance, and then spiritual authority to deal with it. He boldly unmasked the nature, origin, spirit and aim of Elymas' opposition and solemnly invoked the judgment of God, which fell on the sorcerer.

Then, too, *He sustained the missionaries amid opposition and discouragement*, when the Jews in their hostility to Christ expelled them from their territory. The strange and humanly inexplicable sequel to this treatment was, "And the disciples were filled with joy, and with the Holy Spirit".[14] He enabled them to rise above their circumstances and rejoice in the midst of adversity. They found indeed that the Holy Spirit was the divine Comforter.

The First Missionary Council

At the first church council which was held in Jerusalem, *the presence and presidency of the Holy Spirit* were clearly recognized by the assembled delegates. In any matter of doubt, His was the deciding voice. The chairman's wording of the findings of the council was a clear indication of the place accorded to Him in their deliberations: "It seemed good to the Holy Spirit and to us. . . ."[15] He was accorded the place of paramount importance.

The importance the early missionaries attached to the work of the Holy Spirit can be measured by the care with which they introduced new converts and believers to His ministery.[16] Paul traced the ineffectiveness of the twelve disciples of John at Ephesus to their ignorance of the Spirit's filling and empowering.[17] There is a strong case for very early indoctrination of converts in this crucial subject.

When missionaries and mission boards concede to the Holy Spirit the supreme place in their strategy and activities, more spectacular advance will be seen on the mission fields of the world. The fact is, however, that even where His prerogatives are not entirely ignored, He is afforded too little opportunity to display His power.

It was otherwise with Dr. Jonathan Goforth under whose ministry powerful revivals broke out in Korea and China. He was deeply concerned to see revival in his area, and with that end in view he gave himself to an intensive study of the doctrine of the Holy Spirit. He then preached what he had learned to the groups he visited. Deep conviction and confession of sin followed, and an increasing number of conversions.

While speaking to a heathen audience in a Chinese city, Goforth witnessed a stirring in the people's hearts such as he had never seen before. When preaching on the text, "He bore our sins in his own body on the tree",[18] conviction seemed written on every face. When he asked for decisions, practically everyone stood up. Then, turning around seeking one of the ten evangelists who accompanied him to take his place, he found the whole band with a look of awe on their faces. One whispered, "Brother, He for whom we have prayed so long was here in very deed tonight." Everywhere they went in succeeding days, souls sought salvation. They had given the Holy Spirit His rightful place in their work, and reaped their reward in His mighty working in their midst.

REFERENCES

1. John 16:7.   2. John 20:22.   3. Luke 24:14.   4. Acts 2:4.   5. 1 Cor. 12:13.   6. Matt. 24:14.   7. Acts 1:8.   8. Acts 5:3, 4.   9. Acts 13:1-4.   10. Acts 16:6, 7.   11. Acts 15:39.   12. Acts 8:29.   13. Acts 13:9-11.   14. Acts 13:52.   15. Acts 15:28.   16. Acts 8:17, 9:17.   17. Acts 19:26.   18. 1 Pet. 2:24.

Chapter Twelve

SINS AGAINST THE SPIRIT I

"He has set His heart upon accomplishing in us, and for us, the highest possibilities of love and blessing; when we will not yield to His wise and holy will; when we will not let Him educate us, mould us, separate us from the things that weaken and destroy us, and fit us for the weight of glory that He is preparing for us, His heart is vexed, His love is wounded, His purpose is baffled; and if the Comforter could weep, we would see the tears of loving sorrow upon His gentle face."

A. B. SIMPSON

"When sin comes into my life it displeases the Holy Spirit, He reproves me; but let me never forget that it pains Him. He hates sin, and it pains Him because He sees that by sinning I lose His blessing, it does injury to my soul."

EVAN H. HOPKINS

SINS AGAINST THE SPIRIT I

"Grieve not the Holy Spirit."   Eph. 4:30

"Quench not the Spirit."   1 Thess. 5:19

One of the most convincing proofs of the real Personality of the Holy Spirit, is afforded by the character of the offences which men may commit against Him. The importance of this subject may be gauged by the seriousness of the consequences of these sins, whether committed by believer or unbeliever.

The magnitude of an offence is determined, not alone by the nature of the offence, but by the dignity of the one against whom it is committed. In India, a Brahmin could strike a pariah with impunity, but the same offence committed against the Maharajah of the State would be visited with the direst penalty. There is no difference in the nature of the acts, but there is a world of difference between the relative positions and dignity of the persons struck.

So is it with the Holy Spirit. The fact that He is a Divine Person, equal in power and majesty with the Father and the Son, invests every offence committed against Him with special gravity. Indeed, the only sin for which Scripture states that there is no forgiveness is that against the Spirit.

The sins which inflict intense sorrow on the Holy Spirit, fall into two classes. Believers may be guilty of grieving or quenching the Spirit. The unbeliever may blaspheme the Holy Spirit.

I. *Grieving The Spirit*

"Grieve not the Holy Spirit of God."

This expression occurs only once in the New Testament and means "to cause sorrow to". Although this language is anthropathic, it is no mere figure of speech. The fact that we can cause sorrow to the gracious Spirit by our sin should make us sensitive to sin and act as an effective deterrent. But not all Christians realize the poignancy of the sorrow which their sins occasion Him.

"Grieve" is a love word. One can anger an enemy, but not grieve him. The words are mutually exclusive. Only one who loves can be grieved, and the deeper the love the greater the grief. How gracious the Spirit has been to us who have "grieved Him by a thousand falls".

Paul's injunction in this verse may be rendered either, "Cease grieving the Spirit", or "Do not have the habit of grieving the Spirit". If we know of something in our lives which is grieving the Spirit, then we must decisively deal with it, lest we form the tragic habit of grieving the Spirit.

What Grieves the Spirit?

This may be learned from the context of the command, for it occurs in the midst of a list of sins of speech and action, all of which grieve Him. The presence of the Holy Spirit in the believer's body makes it a temple of God, therefore the presence of sin grieves its holy Tenant. It is a healthy exercise to deliberately invite the Spirit's conviction as we go through this list, and discover whether any are present in our lives. It would appear that He is grieved by specific sins, rather than by the presence of sin in the nature.

To be specific, we may grieve Him by *ignoring His indwelling*. Some Christians live as if there were no Holy Spirit. From Sunday morning to Saturday night they give not one thought of conscious recognition to their heavenly Guest. No one appreciates being ignored.

It is possible for enlightened Christians to disregard the Spirit's presence within. Shortly before his death, one of the great Bible teachers said, "Looking back over the past years, I am afraid I have overlooked the Holy Spirit and so have grieved Him." Each day should be marked by a conscious recognition of His presence.

Again, He is grieved when we *infringe His commands*. Only One never grieved Him—the One Who said, "I do always those things that please Him."[1] He was able to do this because He entrusted the government of His life entirely to the Holy Spirit. He was instantly responsive to the Spirit's control.

The temptation in the wilderness is a striking illustration of this fact. "Immediately the Spirit *driveth* Him into the wilderness,"[2] we read. The secret of His life is reflected in the word "driveth". His will was so utterly resigned to the Spirit that He willingly submitted to His control. Unfettered by reluctance or opposition, the Spirit was able to carry out the whole will of God in the body of Christ. He will work similarly in our lives as we submit to His guidance.

Philip was a fine example of sensitivity to the voice of the

Spirit. Engaged as he was in the midst of a flourishing revival, the command, "Arise and go . . . unto Gaza which is desert",[8] must have presented him with a real dilemma. Should he leave the hundreds in the valley of decision and go to a desert? Was it reasonable? Had he refused to respond promptly to the Spirit's pressure, his path would never have crossed that of the influential Ethiopian chancellor.

Since it is the objective of the Spirit to conform us to the image of Christ, anything in which we wilfully depart from the divine ideal is a grief to Him. The word "wilfully" is used advisedly, for sins concerning which our consciences are not enlightened do not grieve the Spirit to the same degree as those which are wilfully committed. The Spirit respects our liberty. When we choose to sin rather than obey His will, He suspends His activity and communion with Christ is broken.

Specific Sins Enumerated

Certain specific sins are especially associated with this injunction.[4] We are to put away *lying*, or whatever is false; to be party to no sham or pretence, whether in word or in deed. *Anger*, too, grieves the Spirit of God, whether manifested as wrath—the sudden surge of feeling, anger with the lid off; or malice—the continuing disposition, anger cooled down to hatred.[5]

True, there is such a thing as sinless anger, for we are exhorted to "be angry and sin not", but it is all too rare. Our sinless Lord blazed with righteous anger at the pious Pharisees who devoured the living of widows.[6] If we are not stirred to anger by moral outrages such as raised His indignation, we are of another spirit. Anger becomes sinful when self-centred. Even justifiable anger may be nursed to such a degree that it degenerates into sin. Personal enmity towards anyone always grieves the Spirit and must not be tolerated.

Dishonesty in every shape and form is to be abjured.[7] In the common mind there are thought to be degrees of honesty, but the Word of God allows no such distinction, "Pilfering" or "purloining" sounds much more respectable than plain "stealing". Petty thefts are considered less serious sins than great mail-train robberies, but the connotation is no different in principle. Stealing is appropriating that to which we have no right. To take wages for work half-done or for time spent in other pursuits is an indirect form of stealing. Meticulous honesty should be the rule of life of the Christian who does not wish to grieve the Spirit.

94

In no way are we more prone to grieve the Spirit than through an unguarded tongue. Hence the apostolic injunction, "Let *no corrupt communication* proceed out of your mouth,"[8] i.e. no speech which is the outcropping of the old carnal nature, the old life. The word means "rotten", "putrid". Some speech reeks with moral corruption, but it must never soil the lips of the Christian. The person who looks around to see who is present before he speaks stands self-condemned. Paul is not emphasizing foul talk alone, but every variety of unprofitable speech. Instead of spreading corruption through his speech, the Christian is to be a channel of grace.

All *bitterness* is to be put away. It is impossible to cherish resentment and bitterness against another without grieving the heavenly Dove. No matter how great the provocation, bitterness is never justified and will harm the one who indulges it more than the one against whom it is directed.

These and kindred sins cause the tender Holy Spirit deep sorrow. When He is ignored, thwarted, disobeyed, when He gives some new revelation of Christ which brings no response, He is grieved.

Can we know?

How may we know if we have grieved Him? This will not be difficult to discern, for the whole spiritual life will be affected. No longer will the Spirit be able to exercise to the full His gracious work in heart and will. The *Bible* will lose its vital grip and *prayer* its joy. It will tend to become a formal duty. The reason is not far to seek. For the illumination of the Scriptures and the inspiration of prayer we are utterly dependent on the One whom we have grieved. Reluctantly His gracious ministry is curtailed, and we are bereft of the help of the only One Who can make Christ and spiritual things a reality.

Victory over sin will be forfeited and will become a wistful memory or a beautiful mirage. The reason is, of course, that it is "the law of the Spirit of life"[9] which makes us free from the law of sin and death.

The realization of *Christ's abiding presence* will fade, for only the Spirit can make His indwelling real to our inner consciousness. *Joy*, the fruit of the Spirit's working, will take to itself wings. Even *assurance of salvation* may be lost through grieving Him who bears witness with our spirits that we are the children of God.[10] *Power* in service will be absent. Salvation is not lost, but usefulness is forfeited.

Does He Withdraw?

What does the Spirit do when we grieve Him? Does He withdraw? Hymnology might lead us to believe that He does.

> *"No more let sin deceive,*
> *Or earthly cares betray;*
> *O may we never, never grieve*
> *The Comforter away."*

But this is not a Biblical conception. Long before the Gift of the Spirit had been bestowed, David prayed, "Take not thy Holy Spirit from me". But He has now come to indwell us and abide forever. When we grieve Him, however, the evidence is that He is regretfully compelled to withdraw His gracious influences and working, and His grief is reflected in the gloom and heaviness of the estranged heart.

If we draw the blind of a room at noonday, the sun still shines without, but we deprive ourselves of its cheering rays. If we wish to again bask in the sun's light and warmth, all we need to do is to raise the blind, and the sun which our action excluded will again flood the room.

When we grieve the Spirit, we draw the blind and exclude His beneficent ministry in our hearts, although He Himself has not withdrawn. We frustrate His desire to reveal Christ in all His sufficiency and grace. Instead, His love compels Him to concentrate on revealing our sin to us until we melt in repentance.

Is there a Remedy?

There is something we can do to enjoy once again the fellowship of the Spirit we have forfeited through our sin. The remedy is simple. "If we confess our sin He is faithful and just to forgive us our sin to cleanse us from all unrighteousness."[11]

Sins, whether of commission or omission which have been committed against God alone, should be confessed to God alone. Sins which have affected another should, wherever possible, be confessed to him as well as to God, and if necessary, apology and restitution be made. Then the Dove of peace will fly back into the heart.

> *"Have I grieved Thy Holy Spirit?*
> *Have I quenched His power within?*
> *If I have, O Lord forgive me:*
> *Cleanse my heart from every sin."*

II. *Quench not the Spirit*

"Quench not the Spirit."[12]

Throughout the Bible the Holy Spirit is frequently alluded to under the symbol of fire. "Quench" carries the significance of putting out a fire, hence the Berkeley Bible rendering, "Do not extinguish the Spirit's fire". It is so used in other connections.[13] Thayer gives its meaning as "to suppress or stifle". This offence, then, would appear to consist in suppressing or stifling the divine flame of the Spirit. The conception is quite appropriate, since He is called "the Spirit of burning",[14] and visibly manifested His empowering presence in the form of "cloven tongues like as of fire",[15] on the day of Pentecost.

From the context it would seem that "quenching" has to do with the Spirit's public work in the Church, and that it relates to service rather than to life. John's prophecy was, "He shall baptize you with the Holy Spirit and with fire,[16] and upon us devolves the responsibility of seeing that this heavenly fire is not quenched by any act of ours.

Writing on this subject, Dr. H. J. Ockenga said: "The informal nature of early Christian worship is described in 1 Cor. 14:23 ff. The Holy Spirit's direction played a very important part in the meetings of worship of the church. The order included a Psalm, a doctrine, a tongue, a revelation and an interpretation, but all was to be done unto edifying. There was to be no restraint upon those who were guided by the Spirit in the midst of the worship. Here we are to avoid two extremes: one is, the reaction against formalism which gives rein to extremes in the attempts of people to follow the Spirit. This repels sincere and cultured persons. On the other hand, there is the impetus to quench all such individual expressions and to resort to a set form of service. Even the Holy Spirit could not break through some of these set forms of service in our churches. It was the intention of Paul to maintain a nice balance between order and opportunity for the Spirit to work. The manifestations of the Spirit's working are not to be despised, nor are they to be courted."

It was probable that some in the church at Thessalonica were trying to put out the fire of the Spirit, especially in the exercise of special gifts, hence the exhortation which follows, "Despise not prophesying".[17] The manifestation of the Spirit in the church or in the individual, whether it be in praise, prayer or prophecy is not to be quenched. It is not difficult to put out the fire of spiritual fervour and zeal.

How May We Quench Him?

We may quench His work in *ourselves* by failing to respond to His calls for service or testimony, or by failure to enter a divinely opened door of opportunity. When worldly methods are substituted for spiritual, when the praise of men is preferred to the praise of God, when service is self-originated rather than God-directed, the Spirit may be quenched.

Fire may be quenched as effectively by neglecting to provide fuel as by dousing it with water. So when the Spirit is denied the necessary fuel which prayer and devout meditation on the Word supply, He is quenched.

A sobering feature of this sin is that we may be guilty of quenching the Spirit *in others* as well as in ourselves.

When the Holy Spirit is given free rein, He will manifest His presence in burning zeal which will set fire to others and will spread like a forest flame. Who does not envy the contagious enthusiasm of the new convert, despite blunders he may make? It is tragically possible, however, for older Christians less zealous and more phlegmatic, to quench the divine flame in his glowing heart by contemptuous words or unsympathetic criticism.

"You should be ashamed of yourself," said an unspiritual elder to an ungifted young man who, at tremendous cost to himself, had given a stumbling testimony for Christ.

"I am ashamed of myself," he rejoined, "but I am not ashamed of my Lord."

The elder came perilously near quenching the Spirit in the heart of that young man.

Again, frivolous conversation after a service in which the Spirit has been present in power may have the same effect.

There is also a sense in which this offence may be referred to the corporate action *of the church*. A church may corporately hinder the work of God and quench the Spirit in His work of salvation and revival. The fires of many an incipient movement of the Spirit have been quenched by divisions, criticism, formalism, boastful advertising, lauding of man, or endeavouring to manipulate the Spirit's operations.

He may be quenched by kindling false fires on the altars of God, "for God will never allow the fire of the Holy Spirit to be mingled with strange fire upon His altars". As Miriam's criticism of Moses, God's appointed leader, arrested the progress of all Israel for seven days, so it is possible for one influential but unspiritual member to paralyse a whole church.

Dr. James Denney contended that "a liturgy, however beautiful, is a melancholy witness to the quenching of the Spirit: it may be better or worse than the prayers of one man, but it could never compare for fervour with the spontaneous prayers of a living church."

REFERENCES

1. John 8:29. 2. Mark 1:12. 3. Acts 8:26. 4. Eph. 4:25–29.
5. Eph. 4:25–29. 6. Matt. 23:14. 7. Eph. 4:28. 8. Eph. 4:29.
9. Rom. 8:2. 10. Rom. 8:16. 11. 1 John 1:9. 12. 1 Thess.
5:19. 13. Matt. 12:20, Mark 9:48. 14. Isa. 4:4. 15. Acts 2:3.
16. Matt. 3:11. 17. 1 Thess. 5:20.

Chapter Thirteen

SINS AGAINST THE SPIRIT II

"For myself I feel, as surely many a Christian does, how very much easier it is to say what this great acme and last development of sin is not than what it is. Whatever it is, it is always and for ever true that the man who as a fact comes repentant to the feet of Christ for pardon finds it. And whatever it is, the Saviour's own words of warning surely imply that it is not, so to speak, a terrible accident of the sinful soul's action, but a development, the result of a process, the outcome of a deliberately formed condition . . .

"Meanwhile let us take heed, watching and praying, not to grieve the Spirit of love and holiness. It is better to be dismayed than to presume. But it is best of all most reverently to trust."

H. C. G. MOULE

"To sin against God under the law was a serious matter. The sin against Jesus Christ in human form was yet more serious (John 15:22); nevertheless the Son in His humility presented Himself in visible form to men; to repulse Him was still pardonable. But to resist the Spirit who glorifies Him and who gives rise within our hearts to an unmistakably clear conviction is an act of wilful sin, willingly and deliberately shutting the door in the face of God. The work of the Spirit, seeking to place within us the Saviour's presence, is the final issue in God's plan for us. If man rejects it and maintains his stubborness, God can do no more for him; He cannot save him in opposition to his will."

RENE PACHE

SINS AGAINST THE SPIRIT II

III. *Blaspheming the Holy Spirit*

> *"Wherefore I say unto you, all manner of sin and blasphemy shall be forgiven unto men; but the blasphemy against the Holy Spirit shall not be forgiven unto men. And whosoever speaketh a word against the Son of Man, it shall be forgiven him; but whosoever speaketh against the Holy Spirit, it shall not be forgiven him, neither in this world, neither in the world to come."*
>
> Matt. 12:31, 32

If the seriousness of a sin is measured by the reach of its consequences, then none is more serious than blasphemy of the Holy Spirit. The subject is confessedly difficult, and extreme dogmatism would be unwarranted, but its great importance demands an attempt to discover the nature of this sin, which, it would appear, irrevocably seals the fate of the one who commits it.

Under the old economy, blaspheming the name of God incurred the death penalty.[1] In the new dispensation, the blasphemy of the Holy Spirit remains the one unpardonable sin. It is the view of some that the sin was that of charging Jesus with doing His miracles *through Satanic power,* and not through the Holy Spirit. It could therefore be committed only so long as our Lord was on earth, and was in fact committed by the Pharisees in their blasphemies.[2]

This view however, does not satisfy all the facts of the case. Christ did not affirm that the Pharisees *had* committed this sin. That they had blasphemed the Son of Man was true, and He was warning them not to take the further fatal step of blaspheming the Spirit.

Others, following St. Augustine, advocate the simpler view that *all who are finally impenitent,* having rejected the offer of God's grace, are guilty of this sin. While this view answers many of the problems involved, it does not explain Christ's statement that there would be no forgiveness for them, either in this world, or in the world to come. It is apparently a sin that can be committed at any time during life, but final impenitence cannot be determined until death.

The third view which we present seems to accord more with the tenor of Scripture. We will endeavour to reach a conclusion by asking and answering several relevant questions.

What is it to Blaspheme?

Blasphemy is contempt or indignity offered to God. It is to revile, slander, speak lightly or amiss of sacred things or Persons. It is a sin not of the lips alone, but issues from the heart.[3] The same word is translated elsewhere as "evil-speaking".[4]

Why is Blaspheming the Spirit more serious than Blaspheming the Son of Man?

Surely not because there is any greater sanctity in one Person of the Godhead than in another. It should be noted that Jesus extended forgiveness for every other sin, however grave, even for blaspheming Himself, the Son of Man. Wherein lies the difference, since both are God? It appears to lie here. Our Lord does not here use the title "Son of God" of Himself, but "Son of Man". The Son of Man is God veiled in humanity, God incognito, God in humiliation. The Holy Spirit is God in majesty. It was against Jesus as Son of Man the Pharisees had blasphemed, for they explicitly refused to accept His claim to be Son of God.[5]

Paul acknowledged that he had blasphemed the Son of Man, but he received forgiveness because he "did it ignorantly in unbelief".[6] There is a marked difference between slandering the Son of Man in His veiled condition, and slandering Him after the Holy Spirit, the Gift of His exaltation, had completely vindicated His claim to deity. Many who doubtless had spoken evil of Jesus in the days of His flesh, when they received the fuller light of the Holy Spirit on the day of Pentecost, became His ardent disciples.

In the midst of the most explicit and comprehensive offer of pardon in all Scripture, there is indicated one fatal exception: "He that shall blaspheme against the Holy Spirit hath NEVER forgiveness," and Matthew adds, "neither in the world to come".

What is this unpardonable Sin?

The views of some noted Bible scholars are of interest.

"Constant and consummate opposition to the influence of the Holy Spirit, because of a deliberate preference of darkness to the light."

A. H. PLUMMER

103

"In order to it, there needs the concurrence of great and God-given light upon good and evil, sin and salvation with a resolved, deliberate and matured hostility and repulsion on the part of the will; a personal hatred of recognized, eternal holiness."

H. C. G. MOULE

"A combination of clear intellectual knowledge of the gospel, with deliberate rejection of it and wilful choice of sin; the union of light in the head and hatred in the heart."

J. C. RYLE

"A persistent and continuous attitude of deliberate and wilful sin against light, maintained in the face of all God's efforts to bring about a change."

W. H. G. THOMAS

"The full personal rejection of all the moral demand which the Holy Spirit makes through the conscience."

L. H. CURTIS

It will be noted that these scholars are in essential agreement on the following points:

It is *not a sin of ignorance,* but a sin against spiritual knowledge and light. God has not set a mysterious line over which one may unwittingly cross.

It is *not an isolated act,* but a habitual attitude, a sin in character, crystallized in opposition to God.

It is *a sin of the heart,* and not merely of the intellect or tongue—not an unbidden thought or unpremeditated word.

It is *a sin committed in wilful resistance* to the strivings of the Spirit, a sin of presumption.

Who is Guilty of this Sin?

Many who harbour morbid fears of having committed this sin—and they are very many in number—should find comfort in the foregoing considerations. If this sin is, as we believe it to be, a wilful and persistent closing of the eyes against the light and the ears against the truth, then the fact that one is distressed at the thought of having committed it, is clear proof that he has not done so. Had the sin been committed, there would have been a cessation of sensibility, a spiritual deadness and indifference. Conscience would be seared and unresponsive, and the Spirit's strivings silenced.

If a person persistently continues in resistance to the Spirit, it is God Who in turn hardens their heart, by withdrawing the gentle strivings of the Holy Spirit. Belief then becomes impossible. "Then they could not believe, because that Esaias said again, He hath blinded their eyes and hardened their hearts; that they should not see with their eyes, nor understand with their heart, and be converted, and I would heal them."[7]

But this condition must be distinguished from *backsliding*. A true child of God may backslide and commit grievous sin. He will, however, despite his sins and failures, give proof of his possession of the divine life by sooner or later returning to his Saviour in contrition and confession.[8] Those who are deeply convicted of their sin and have a sincere desire to return to the Lord, give evidence by these very facts that they are not guilty of this sin, for they are clear marks of the working of the Holy Spirit.

Why is there no Forgiveness for this Sin?

Is it because there is not sufficient virtue in the blood of Christ to cleanse it? Is it because God is capricious? Assuredly not. There must always be two parties to forgiveness—the forgiver, and the one needing forgiveness. If the one who has sinned obstinately refuses to be forgiven, what more can God do? For His Spirit to continue to strive would only increase the responsibility of the sinning man to no purpose. The sin is unforgivable, because it rejects forgiveness, and for such there is no further provision. It is unforgivable, because it is "an eternal sin",[9] and its punishment unending, because the sin is unending.

Concerning the unpardonable sin, Dr. Joseph Parker said, "Explanations of this mystery there are probably none. It best explains itself by exciting a holy fear as to trespass." Any who have not yet responded to the wooings of the Spirit, should cease to gamble on the goodness of God, and yield to Him at once.

REFERENCES

1. Lev. 24:15–16. 2. Matt. 12:24. 3. Matt. 15:19. 4. Eph. 4:31. 5. Matt. 12:24. 6. 1 Tim. 1:13. 7. John 12:39, 40. 8. 1 John 1:9. 9. Mark 3:29 RSV.

Chapter Fourteen

THE GIFTS OF THE SPIRIT I

"It was in the full sense of the word a communion of the Spirit which consisted in a continuous and incredibly intensified enthusiasm, in an inspiration which exalted every faculty to the manifestation of miracle even in the natural domain. To this Spirit nothing was impossible. He found utterance in ecstatic speech, imparted hidden mysteries, and made prophets and teachers of the uncultured. He inspired every sort of manifestation of ministering love, of guiding wisdom, of self-sacrificing devotion. He performed miracles, healed diseases, moved mountains, and transformed men who felt themselves miserable and depressed, into a cloud of witnesses overflowing with strength and courage."

VON DOBSCHUTZ

"The Church is the Body of Christ and the characteristic of a healthy body is that every part in it performs its own function for the good of the whole. But unity does not mean uniformity, and therefore within the Church, there are differing gifts and differing functions; but every one of them is the gift of the same Spirit, and every one of them is designed, not for the glory of the individual member of the Church, but for the good of the whole."

WILLIAM BARCLAY

THE GIFTS OF THE SPIRIT I

"There are diversities of gifts but the same Spirit."

1 Cor. 12:4

"The Spirit divideth (gifts) to every man severally as He will."

1 Cor. 12:11

The first concern of the ascended Lord appears to have been the equipment of His infant church for its inevitable conflict with the powers of darkness. "When He ascended up on high, He led captivity captive and gave gifts unto men."[1] These gifts He bestowed through His Spirit, and it is through His working that they function. Only supernatural gifts would suffice for warfare against a supernatural foe. Without such gifts, the Church would be little more than any other social institution.

Gift and Gifts

A clear distinction is to be observed between the Gift of the Spirit and the gifts of the Spirit. The former was bestowed on the Church in answer to the prayer of Christ and in fulfilment of the promise of the Father. The latter are bestowed on individual believers as and when the Spirit in His sovereignty pleases.

On the day of Pentecost, fifty days after the resurrection, the great gift of the Spirit was poured out on the waiting Jewish Christians. Later, in the house of Cornelius the Gentiles, too, became beneficiaries. The gift of the Spirit is for every member of the Body of Christ without discrimination,[2] while the gifts of the Spirit are special and bestowed individually.[3] The gift is absolute and for ever,[4] but the gifts may atrophy through disuse.

Though completed on God's side, the gift of the Spirit awaited and awaits the appropriation of individual believers. Many are unaware that the Spirit has been given in this sense, and since a gift is not effective until received, the purpose of the divine benevolence is not achieved. Our hymnology is often faulty in petitioning God to give His Spirit, as though he had never been given. We rightly pray for a greater manifestation of His power in our lives and ministry, but the gift has already been made to all, once and for all.

Gifts and Fruit

A similar discrimination should be made between the gifts and the fruit of the Spirit. Nine gifts are enumerated,[5] while the fruit is depicted in nine qualities of character.[6] Between the two there are several clear contrasts.

A gift may be imparted from without, and may remain separate and distinct. Fruit however is not an extraneous addition to a tree, but the issue of its life, and is produced from within. Fruit is a quality of character which may be produced in every life, but not so the gifts. They are special, and are distributed as the Spirit chooses, so as to fit the individual for the function he has to fulfil in the body of Christ.

There is no several distribution of fruit, but there may be with the gifts. It is recorded that "He gave some, apostles; and some, prophets; and some, evangelists",[7] but there is no parallel statement that He gave to some love, to some joy and to some peace. Gifts are in the plural, but the fruit is in the singular number, for the fruit is the product of the working of the Holy Spirit in the whole man.

Of the Corinthian Christians Paul wrote that they "came behind in no gift,[8] but they lagged far behind in the fruit of the Spirit. The presence of such fruit in the life is a far more reliable evidence of spirituality than is the possession and exercise of spectacular spiritual gifts. Our Lord indicated an infallible test, "By their fruits ye shall know them".[9] Satan can counterfeit and imitate spiritual gifts, but he is baffled in trying to imitate the fruit of the Spirit.

Signification of Spiritual Gifts

Two words are used of these gifts which, taken together afford helpful insight into their true nature. They are *pneumatika* and *charismata*.[10] In 1 Cor. 12:1 "gifts", is in italics, and the word signifies simply "something of or from the Spirit". G. Campbell Morgan translates the word, "spiritualities". The Corinthian church was plagued with carnalities and needed to return to the spiritualities, that which has its source in the Spirit.

In 1 Cor. 12:4 "charismata" signifies "gifts of grace". They are bestowed altogether apart from human merit or deserts. The

109

two words taken together indicate that these gifts are extraordinary powers and enduements bestowed by the Spirit upon individual believers as equipment for Christian service and the edification of the Church, and that they are given sovereignly and undeserved. They are distinct from the natural powers of man.

The gifts of the Spirit may be classified roughly as follows:

(a) Gifts which *qualify their possessors for the ministry of the Word:* Apostleship, prophecy, teaching, shepherding, evangelism, knowledge and wisdom, kinds of tongues, interpretation of tongues, discerning of spirits.[11]

(b) Gifts which *equip their possessors to render services of a practical nature:* miracles, healing, administration, ruling, helps.

It is not as in nature that only few are gifted. Every man has some gift. "The manifestation of the Spirit is given to *every man.*" This does not mean that everyone is exercising the gift or gifts with which the Spirit has endowed him. Nor does everyone necessarily know what his gift is. But it is clear that every Christian has been allotted at least one gift which he is to exercise for the upbuilding of the Church.

The metaphor employed is that of a body and its members. Each member is indispensable to the full functioning of the whole body. The most obscure church member is as necessary as the most prominent. Each has a distinct and separate ministry for which the Spirit has gifted him. All gifts are to be evaluated in the light of the common good. If we were left to our own choice of gifts, what confusion there would be! The body of Christ would be a monstrosity.

Purpose of the Gifts

They are not bestowed for the self-aggrandizement of the recipient, or as an evidence of a special enduement of the Spirit, but for the profit and edification of the Body of Christ. The possessor is only the instrument and not the receiver of the glory. "Each of us is just a pen in the hand of God," said Richard Baxter, "and what honour is there in a pen?" The gift is for ministry to others, "for the perfecting of the saints, for the work of the ministry, for the edifying of the Body of Christ".[12]

The nature of the gifts indicates that they are for the most part gifts of service. Not one of them directly concerns character. They are God's equipment and enabling for effective service.

In the early days of the Church they served another purpose.

110

They were necessary as the divine credentials of the apostles in their testimony to the resurrection of Christ. Who would believe the word of these "ignorant and unlearned men" with their fantastic story of a man who rose from the dead? They were not left unaccredited, however, for "God bore them witness, both with signs and wonders, and with divers miracles and gifts of the Holy Spirit".[13]

This co-witness of God afforded clear evidence to the unbelieving Jews that the promised Holy Spirit had indeed been given and was exercising His divine prerogatives. Once the credibility of the witness of the apostles had been established, and the canon of the New Testament had been completed, there was not the same necessity for the exercise of the miraculous gifts which gradually became less prominent. Bishop H. C. G. Moule said in this connection: "It is not ours to be decisive where the Scripture is reticent. But on the whole Scripture points to a cessation of *charismata* in the normal life of the church. . . . In 1 Cor. 13:8 there is the intimation of a certain transiency in these manifestations, in contrast to the permanency of grace."

There are those who contend that the miraculous gifts completely passed away, but this would be difficult to maintain in the light of church and missionary history.

Diversities of Gifts

Through the one Spirit are mediated divine gifts.[14] A musician cannot produce harmonious melody from a single note, or an artist a masterpiece with one colour. Similarly the Spirit's manifold purpose for the Church can be accomplished only by means of several gifts. No one gift is common to all Christians, nor does one Christian possess all gifts. On the other hand, no Christian has been passed over by the Holy Spirit in His distribution. There are no useless organs in the Body of Christ. Each has some function.

Paul's metaphor of the body illustrates the fact that not all the gifts are spectacular or such as would command public attention. As the body is not all tongue, so it is not necessary for all believers to possess outstanding powers of speech. So with every other gift. Of the one hundred and twenty in the upper room on the day of Pentecost, most were never heard of again. They doubtless returned to their homes to be humble yet obscure witnesses to Christ. Only a few received spiritual gifts that fitted them for more prominent public ministry.

Frequently though not always, the gifts bestowed accord with natural talents and endowments, but they always transcend them. Spiritual gifts pertain to the spiritual birth of Chritsians, not their natural birth. They are supernatural, but make use of and increase the natural abilities possessed.

The explanation of the widely differing capabilities of equally devoted and Spirit-controlled Christians lies in the fact that the gifts are adapted to the ministry to which the recipient is called, to the place he is to fulfil in the Body of Christ. Just as in a family there is a diversity of gifts—one being musical, another mechanical, another artistic—so is it in the heavenly family. All derive their life from the Spirit, but not all inherit the same gifts.

Gradation of Gifts

Paul urged the Corinthian Christians, "Covet earnestly the best gifts" or "the greater gifts",[15] as many older manuscripts have it. This does not imply that more honour attaches to the possession of one gift than to another. The exhortation is immediately followed by the revelation of something yet more desirable than even these higher gifts—heavenly love.[16] In his exhortation, "Desire spiritual gifts", the gift of prophecy is urged to be given primacy. Just as some spiritual gifts bring most edification to the Church, and these are the ones to be desired. The question is one of practical use rather than of superiority. Those gifts are best and highest which issue in ministry of the Word, the capacity to transmit the message of God.

The gifts, then, are not all of equal value, but are graduated. Paul recognized such a distinction. "Greater is he that prophesieth than he that speaketh with tongues."[17] In his list of gifts, he specifically sets them in order of importance. "First ... secondarily ... thirdly ... after that ... then ..."[18] Let us be careful not to put first that which God has put last.

Sovereignty in Bestowal of Gifts

Especially among immature Christians, there is the danger of being envious of the gifts of others. Young men often expect to become Moodys or Spurgeons or Grahams as the result of some critical spiritual experience, and are disheartened when no such spectacular change takes place. The lesson to be mastered is that we cannot dictate to the Spirit in His administration. His will is sovereign and final. It is the giver who has the right to select the gift. He sets us as members in the body "as it has pleased Him",[19] and our place in the body will determine the nature of the gift we receive from Him. There is therefore no grounds for envying another. We are exhorted to covet earnestly the greater gifts, but this surely requires that we carefully and diligently cultivate those we already possess. In this way our capacity will be increased so that we can be entrusted with yet greater gifts.

Speaking of his own experience, Samuel Chadwick, the great Methodist preacher of an earlier generation said, "I think I was rather dull, a little slow, delicate in health, never allowed to play an open-air game since I was born until I was grown up, and then I pleased myself! There was nothing that indicated anything but a very earnest, plodding, determined youth who was converted when he was a boy. He had a sure call to preach when he was a lad. It was an impossible call so far as any human element could discern, but God thrust me out into the work, and gave me my first job to fill an empty chapel.

"I was up against a great problem for which I had no solution. When I was twenty-three I had been preaching about seven years, and had fifteen sermons. They were all I had got, but I had the satisfaction of knowing they were all my own, and they had been born of much travail and many tears. I thought those fifteen sermons would turn the world upside down. When I had preached them, there were not fifteen more people in the chapel than when I had started. When I was confronted with this proposition, God enlightened my conscience and opened my eyes to the need of some reinforcement of power."

He then described the experience which followed his reception of the filling of the Spirit. "What happened was this. Every part of my being wakened up. I did not get a new set of brains but I got a new mentality. I did not get a new faculty of speech, but I got a new effectiveness of speech. I did not get a new dictionary, but a new Bible. Immediately I was a new creature, with the same basis of natural qualities, vitalized, energized, quickened, reinforced into a bigger vitality and effectiveness that nobody would ever have dreamed possible. That is what happens to those upon whom the Spirit comes."

May Gifts be Lost?

This perplexing problem is sooner or later faced by every Christian worker. He meets people living obviously carnal lives who are exercising spiritual gifts, and apparently with resultant blessing. Men who are great preachers or hold high office in the

Church yet whose private lives belie their profession sometimes seem to meet with more success than others whose lives are godly and consistent. What is the explanation?

If spiritual gifts were the outcome of the filling of the Spirit, or if they were dependent on the continuance of this experience, they would automatically disappear when tolerated sin grieved the Holy Spirit. It would seem, however, that they are bestowed at regeneration, and their continued exercise is not dependent on a high plane of Christian living, as for example in the case of the highly-gifted but corrupt and divided Corinthian church. Samson continued to perform mighty feats for a long time after he was out of touch with God.

Perhaps some light is shed on the subject by Paul's words: "The gifts and call of God are irrevocable"[20] or, "God never goes back on His gifts or call."[21] Marvin Vincent says the idea conveyed in the words "without repentance" is, "not subject to recall". Without dogmatism it is suggested that for this reason the continued possession of spiritual gifts is no criterion of the spiritual state of the possessor, whether it be oneself or another. It would seem that while sin inevitably affects the production of the fruit of the Spirit, it does not affect the gifts to the same degree

REFERENCES

1. Eph. 4:8. 2. Acts 2:38. 3. 1 Cor. 12:11. 4. John 14:16. 5. 1 Cor. 12:8–10. 6. Gal. 5:22–23. 7. Eph. 4:11. 8. 1 Cor. 1:7. 9. Matt. 7:16. 10. 1 Cor. 12:1, 4. 11. Rom. 12:6–8, 1 Cor. 12:4–11, 28–30; Eph. 4:7–12. 12. Eph. 4:12. 13. Heb. 2:4. 14. 1 Cor. 12:4. 15. 1 Cor. 12:31. 16. 1 Cor. 14:1. 17. 1 Cor. 14:5. 18. 1 Cor. 12:28. 19. 1 Cor. 12:18. 20. Rom. 11:29 Moffatt. 21. Rom. 11:29 RSV.

Chapter Fifteen

THE GIFTS OF THE SPIRIT II

"Everyone has some gift, therefore all should be encouraged.
No one has all gifts, therefore all should be humble.
All gifts are for the one Body, therefore all should be harmonious.
All gifts are from the Lord, therefore all should be contented.
All gifts are mutually helpful and needful, therefore all should be studiously faithful.
All gifts promote the health and strength of the whole Body, therefore none can be safely dispensed with.
All gifts depend on His fulness for power, therefore all should keep in close touch with Him."

ARTHUR T. PIERSON

THE GIFTS OF THE SPIRIT II

"And He gave some, apostles; and some, prophets; and some, pastors and teachers; for the perfecting of the saints, for the work of the ministry, for the edifying of the body of Christ."

Eph. 4:11–12

"Having then gifts differing according to the grace that is given to us...."

Rom. 12:6

In referring to the gifts within the Church, Paul differentiates between those which are given to individual men, and the spiritually gifted men who are given to the Church. In Ephesians he enumerates five orders of ministry given to the churches for their upbuilding. In Corinthians and Romans he deals rather with the spiritual gifts themselves.

It is not clear exactly how many gifts there are, since some appear to impinge on others, so we will consider those which may be easily classified.

Gifted Men

Apostles

First in order of importance are apostles. This term is not confined to the Twelve, but it would seem that to be an apostle one must have seen Jesus,[1] and have been a witness of the resurrection.[2] He must also have been called by Christ or by the Holy Spirit, as was Barnabas.[3] Apostles were endued with miraculous powers as credentials of their office. James, our Lord's brother was an apostle,[4] and so were Andronicus and Junia,[5] Silvanus[6] and others. These qualifications for apostleship meant that they were an order bound to die out. The Church is built upon the *foundation* of the apostles and prophets.

The apostle was, literally, "a delegate, a messenger, one sent forth with orders". (Thayer). According to J. C. Lambert, "The apostolate was not a limited circle of officials holding a well-defined position of authority in the Church, but a large class of men who discharged one—and that the highest—of the functions of the prophetic ministry."⁷

The more generally accepted view, however, is that the word is used in the New Testament in a twofold sense. First in a restricted sense as the official name of Christ's twelve chosen disciples, who saw Him after the resurrection and laid the foundations of His Church. Second, in a broader, unofficial sense as designating accredited Christian messengers, commissioned by a church community, as was Barnabas.⁸

The apostles did not serve a merely local church, but their authority ran throughout the whole Church.

Prophets

It appears that the New Testament prophet like the apostle, ministered to the Church at large, not to a local congregation. His function was more that of a proclaimer than a predicter, more a forth-teller than a fore-teller, although the latter element was not entirely absent, e.g. the prophecy of Agabus.⁹

The essential mark of prophecy is that in it God's voice is heard, for it is inspired speech. The emphasis is not on prediction, but on setting forth what God has said. The prophet was moved to utter the deep things of God, and spoke "to edification, and exhortation and comfort". Since prophecy is God's message, it will always have deep significance, never be trifling or trite, and will always be in keeping with the written Word. It was the gift most to be coveted.¹⁰ Spirit empowered preaching would probably be the nearest present-day equivalent.

Evangelists

The evangelist, one who announced Good News, possessed the special gift of preaching the gospel message so effectively that souls were brought into the experience of salvation. It was the evangelist who founded the churches, while pastors and teachers built them up. Like the prophet, in the early Church the evangelist had a roving ministry among the unconverted. He did not enjoy the prestige of the apostle or prophet. While all are not called to the special *office* of evangelist, all are called, like Timothy, to do the work of an evangelist.¹¹ The function of the evangelist was somewhat similar to that of our pioneer missionary. His work was not necessarily confined to preaching the way of salvation, but included the establishing of converts and gathering them into congregations.

Pastors

The word *pastor* comes from a root meaning "to protect", hence, "shepherd". The verbal form was used by our Lord in His recommissioning of Peter;[12] by Peter in writing to other ministers;[13] and by Paul to the elders at Ephesus.[14] He groups pastors and teachers together, probably because these two gifts are so often found in association. Since it is the responsibility of the shepherd to feed his flock, the two gifts complement each other. It is less common to find these two gifts possessed by an evangelist.

The pastor's role is to lead, feed and care for his flock, and so far as he is able, to protect them from hostile influences. This is an exacting ministry which makes heavy draughts on his compassion and patience. He must carry his people on his heart and feed them with the truth of God.

The need of men with this gift is the more apparent when it is remembered that in those days the Christian Church was only "a little island in the sea of paganism".

Teachers

This is one of the major gifts of the Spirit to the Church. The teacher's function was to interpret the Word of God to His flock. Teaching, in this sense, was the supernatural ability to explain and apply the truths received from God for the Church. The teacher did not originate his own message, but through study and the Spirit's illumination made divine truth clear to his people. His gift was distinct from that of the prophet who spoke as the direct mouthpiece of God.

According to William Barclay, the teacher had a dual function. In the absence of a written record, they were repositories of the gospel story for the early Church. Most of the new Christians came direct from heathenism, and were utterly ignorant of Christianity. To them the teacher had to explain the great doctrines of the faith. While their role is not in all respects the same today, the true teacher plays a vital part in the growth of the Church.

Spiritual Gifts

Among the extraordinary powers bestowed on individuals for the edification of the Church, were

The Word of Wisdom, and
The Word of Knowledge.[15]

The word, or utterance of *wisdom* is the outcome of direct
insight into spiritual truth, the knowledge of God and His ways
which comes not so much from study as from communion.
Clement of Alexandria defined wisdom as "the knowledge of
things human and divine, and of their causes". The utterances
of one possessing this endowment, are full of God's wisdom.

The utterance of *knowledge* is more practical, the application
of the divine *wisdom* to daily life. Both gifts are not necessarily
combined in the one person. Many erudite people lack wisdom.

Faith[16]

Saving faith is not in view here, for though it is the gift of
God, it is not a *special* gift of the Spirit. It is rather wonder-
working faith, the faith that can remove mountains.[17] The
context supports this view. It is the special gift of faith bestowed
in order to enable its possessor to carry out a special ministry.
George Muller, for example, possessed this gift to a unique
degree, but many less known people have possessed and exercised this gift—the faith that turns vision into fact.

Gifts of Healing[18]

This gift is the supernatural intervention of God through a
human instrument, to restore health to the body. It is acts of healing that are in view. Although the incidence of the gift of
healing has waned, it would seem that it has never entirely
disappeared from the Church. It is unfortunate that there have
been great frauds and abuses perpetrated in the name of the
gift.

From the Scripture it would appear that the gift was not
effective in every case, but only according to God's sovereign
will. Scripture holds out no blanket promise that every sickness
will be healed. Paul, though he possessed the gift, was unable
to heal Trophimus and had to leave him sick.[19] Instead of
healing Timothy, he advised medication for his frequent indis-
position.[20]

Working of Miracles[21]

The word "miracles" is really, "powers", a display of power,
the ability to go beyond the natural. It is often used of the

miracles of Jesus.[22] As the phrase is preceded by the word "another", this gift would appear to refer to miracles other than healing. Examples would be, the death of Ananias and Sapphira, the smiting of Elymas, the exorcism of demons, the miraculous powers mentioned in Mark 16:17.

The late Professor Christlieb of Bonn in a most original and interesting discussion of miracles wrote: "The work of missions is outwardly, at least, more extended than it ever was before. In this region, therefore, according to our former rule, miracles should not be entirely wanting. Nor are they. We cannot, therefore, fully admit the proposition that no more miracles are performed in our day. In the history of modern missions we find many wonderful occurrences which unmistakably remind us of the apostolic age. In both periods there are similar hindrances to be overcome, and similar palpable confirmations of the Word are needed to convince the dull sense of men." If miraculous happenings sometimes occur in missionary work today, it is largely because in those areas conditions closely resemble those faced by the early church. In countries long enlightened by the gospel, miracles are not so necessary. This is a realm in which we cannot dictate to the sovereignty of God.

Discerning of spirits[23]

This is the ability to discriminate between different kinds of spirits, to distinguish the spurious from the true, the spirit of truth from the spirit of error.[24] So long as there was no written New Testament, this gift was of special importance, for it enabled the possessor to distinguish between the psychic and the physical, the divine and the demonic, false teaching from the true.

The Spirit enables him to tell whether the professed gifts were really from Him and supernatural, or were merely strange though natural, or even diabolical. The exhortation of John to "test the spirits"[25] had this in view, and is still very relevant today when there is so much that is false yet persuasive in the form of cults and heresies.

Helps[26]

The gift of "helps" or "ministering" is in essence giving help and assistance to those in need. The verb is used by Paul in writing to the Ephesian believers: "I have showed you all things, how that so labouring ye ought to *support* the weak."[27] It may have special reference to the work of deacons. There is wide scope for the exercise of this ministry amongst the poor, sick, aged, orphans and widows. There is more than mere general helpfulness in view. It is rather a *special*, Spirit-given ability to help in such cases. It is a gift that affords endless scope to those who desire to serve the Lord, yet possess no special gift of utterance.

Governments and Ruling[28]

The term "governments" which occurs only here, is the word for the steersman of a ship, who guides it through rocks and shoals to harbour. The word "rulers", means "the one standing in front", or the leader. In any work of God, leadership and a certain amount of administration are necessary, and the Spirit imparts special gifts for this work. It is work that is unspectacular and demanding, and not always appreciated. Nevertheless it is necessary to the smooth functioning of the work of the Kingdom.

In Romans 12 Paul adds some other gifts to those already mentioned which deserve brief notice.

Exhortation[29] is the ability to stir people to act on truth preached and received. The dominating note of exhortation should be encouragement to put God and His truth to the test.

Giving[30] can be a special gift bestowed as well as a grace cultivated.[31] It is the desire and ability to use temporal possessions for the highest good of man and the greater glory of God. Robert Le Tourneau is a modern example of one with this special gift. It is not confined to those who possess great wealth.

Showing mercy[32] is a gift, and the term is variously rendered in modern versions, e.g. "He who shows pity", "If you are helping others in distress", "He who does acts of mercy". Each rendering sheds some light on its significance. To be effective, this gift must be exercised with kindliness and cheerfulness, not as a matter of duty.

There is no suggestion that the list of gifts of the Spirit referred to in this chapter is exhaustive. The gifts of tongues and interpretation of tongues are treated separately.

REFERENCES

1. 1 Cor. 9 : 1. 2. Acts 1 : 22. 3. Acts 14 : 4, 7. 4. Gal. 1 : 19. 5. Rom. 16 : 7. 6. 1 Thess. 2 : 6. 7. 1 Cor. 12 : 28, Eph. 4 : 11. 8. Acts 13 : 3.

9. Acts 11:27, 28.   10. 1 Cor. 14:1, 19, 22.   11. 2 Tim. 2:5.
12. John 21:16.   13. 1 Pet. 5:2.   14. Acts 20:28.   15. 1 Cor.
12:8.   16. 1 Cor. 12:9.   17. 1 Cor. 13:2.   18. 1 Cor. 12:9, 28, 30.
19. 2 Tim. 4:20.   20. 1 Tim. 5:23.   21. 1 Cor. 12:10.   22. Mark
5:30.   23. 1 Cor. 12:28.   24. 1 John 4:6.   25. 1 Tim. 4:1, John 4:1.
26. 1 Cor. 12:28.   27. Acts 20:25.   28. 1 Cor. 12:28.   29. Rom.
12:8.   30. Rom. 12:8.   31. 2 Cor. 8:7.   32. Rom. 12:8.

Chapter Sixteen

THE GIFT OF TONGUES

"The Corinthians had apparently used the gifts as a means of fomenting division. They regarded the possession of such gifts as a matter for pride, and set up one against another on the basis of the possession or otherwise of this gift or that gift. Paul insists that this is the wrong attitude. Though he recognizes that there is diversity in the endowments conferred by the Spirit, yet it is *the same Spirit*. The Spirit does not fight against Himself. The gifts He gives to one are to set forward the same Divine purpose as the different gifts He gives to another."

LEON MORRIS

THE GIFT OF TONGUES

"They all began to speak with other tongues."

Acts 2:4

"To another, divers kinds of tongues."

1 Cor. 12:10

At the commencement of this chapter on one gift of the Spirit that has both ardent advocates and acrid adversaries, let it be stated that the sole object in view is to clarify the Scripture teaching on the subject, and not to espouse a special view. An honest endeavour has been made to attain objectivity. If the reader detects no ardent advocacy of the pursuit of this gift in our times, it is because that seems to be consonant with Paul's treatment of the subject. On the other hand, the position is not taken that there can be no genuine gift of tongues in this day.

The phenomena accompanying the descent of the Spirit on the day of Pentecost bore clear witness to the release of a new spiritual power, the dawning of a new era. The assembled crowds were confounded by the spectacular gift of speaking with other tongues which the Spirit had imparted to the waiting disciples. All were greatly impressed by the fact that every man heard the disciples speak in his own language. "They were all amazed and marvelled."[1]

What was the Pentecostal Gift?

What was "the promise of the Father?"[2] for which the disciples were commanded to wait in Jerusalem? It was the "enduement of power from on high". The gift of tongues, like the sound as of wind, and tongues as of fire, was incidental. The two things are distinct and separable. The evidence of the enduement was effectiveness and extensiveness in witness.[3] It is true the filling of the Spirit was accompanied by speaking with tongues, but this was neither the gift itself, nor its most significant evidence.

Other Tongues and Unknown Tongues

It is important to discover whether the "other tongues" of

124

Pentecost and the "unknown tongues" at Corinth are identical. Incidentally the word "unknown" does not occur in the Greek. It would be more correctly translated simply, "tongues". "Other tongues" occurs only in Acts 2:4. In Acts 10:46 and 19:6 the rendering is simply "with tongues", and in the latter passage, the addition of "and prophesied" would seem to make a distinction between ecstatic utterance and plainly spoken teaching.

It is the view of E. H. Plumptre that, apart from the day of Pentecost, the tongues were not "the power of speaking in a language which had not been learned in the common way of learning, but the ecstatic utterance of rapturous devotion". His contention has much Scriptural support.

While there may be some correspondences, there are strong contrasts between the tongue-speaking at Pentecost and that at Corinth.

At Pentecost *all* spoke in tongues.[4]

This was not true of the believers at Corinth.[5]

At Pentecost the tongues were understood by all.[6]

At Corinth they were understood by none.[7]

At Pentecost they spoke to men.[8]

At Corinth they spoke to God.[9]

At Pentecost no interpreter was necessary.[10]

At Corinth tongue-speaking was forbidden if no interpreter was present.[11]

At Pentecost tongues were a sign or credential to believers.[12]

At Corinth it was a sign to unbelievers.[13]

At Pentecost strangers were filled with awe and marvelled.[14]

At Corinth Paul warned that strangers would say they were mad.[15]

At Pentecost there was perfect harmony.[16]

At Corinth there was confusion.[17]

Since there is such a marked difference between these two manifestations of the gift of tongues, it would not be sound exegesis to build a system of doctrine on the identity of the two occurrences.

If the "tongues" of 1 Corinthians 14 are not identical with those of Acts 2, what were they? The "other tongues" of Pentecost were other than their native tongues. They spoke in languages they had not acquired, yet they were real languages which were understood by strangers from other lands who knew them. It was not jargon, but intelligible language. Without dogmatism, it would seem that the tongues of 1 Cor. 14 were ecstatic, vocal utterances, fervent and rapturous religious expressions, not necessarily intelligible to speaker or hearer except through the gift of interpretation. This interpretation of the relevant passages appears to be in harmony with the whole teaching of the chapter.

Can there be Genuine Tongues Today?

Spiritual and scholarly men are ranged on both sides of this question, but it is of vital importance that we endeavour to discover for ourselves the Biblical answer. One school of thought maintains that this gift was temporary, to meet special conditions in the early days of the Church and before there was a written New Testament. This necessity has passed and therefore the gift has been withdrawn.

Be that as it may, he would be a bold man who would, without the clearest and most indisputable Biblical evidence, assert that the Holy Spirit cannot, if He chooses, revive the gift of tongues in our day, even though it may have lapsed through the centuries. There does not appear to be any clear statement in the New Testament that the gift has been withdrawn, or that it may not recur.

It is generally admitted that it is impossible for anyone to prove experimentally that genuine speaking in tongues *cannot* occur today. In the absence of categorical Scriptural guidance, we can only offer an opinion as to the probability or improbability of what God will or will not do.

It appears to the author that the argument against the possibility of a recurrence of genuine tongue-speaking today rests on reasonable inferences rather than on clear statements of Scripture. Proponents of that view argue, as does J. F. Walvoord, that the gift "is not essential to God's purpose now, and that there are good reasons to believe that most, if not all the phenomena which are advanced as proof of modern speaking in tongues is either psychological or demonic activity".

Four lines of argument are adduced to substantiate that tongue-speaking was a *temporary gift* which has now lapsed.

1. There is no record of speaking in tongues before Pentecost. If it began at Pentecost, it can be withdrawn at the divine pleasure. (But surely it can also be revived at the divine pleasure.)

2. Tongues had the characteristic of being a sign to Israel to

prove that the gospel message was from God. As the fulfilment has been established, the sign is no longer needed.

3. Some other spiritual gifts are temporary, e.g. Apostleship.

4. It is predicted that tongues would cease.[18] It was a temporary provision of God for the apostolic period.

It is further argued that in Eph. 4:8–16, chronologically the latest catalogue of gifts, the miracle gifts are omitted. They were needed only while revelation was incomplete.[19] Being the accompaniments of immaturity, they passed away with the attaining of maturity.

It will be noted that there are no categorical statements of Scripture to which one can appeal as the end of all argument, although there is some cogency in the deductions made.

On the other hand, several unequivocal Scriptural statements can be advanced against the argument. Paul's counsel is "Forbid not to speak with tongues".[20] "I thank God that I speak with tongues more than ye all,"[21] he stated; and again, "I would that ye all spoke in tongues."[22] These last two statements, however, should not be divorced from their context. In neither case is it an *unqualified* statement. The first is qualified by the succeeding clause: "I would that ye all spoke in tongues, *but rather* that ye may prophesy." The second also is qualified by the following clause: "I thank God that I speak in tongues more than ye all, *nevertheless* in the church I *would rather* speak five words with my mind ... than ten thousand words in a tongue."

However, to class *all* speaking with tongues as spurious or demonic would be very daring, as it would virtually deny to the Spirit the right to revive the gift at His pleasure.

That there is much that is spurious, and that some tongue-speaking might be classed as jargon or hysteria would be admitted by the more responsible advocates of the gift.

That the gift may be abused is also true, but that is not an argument against its validity so much as a reason for correcting the abuses, as counselled by Paul.

That it is dangerously open to counterfeit and exploitation is also true. But these are not adequate grounds for denying the possibility of God bestowing the gift in our day.

Value of Tongue-speaking

It is axiomatic that this gift when bestowed by the Spirit had real value, and was necessary to the growth and development of the infant Church.

The fact that the Spirit bestowed the gift is sufficient evidence that at least in its pristine purity, and when exercised within the divinely ordained restrictions, it was neither unnecessary nor useless. Otherwise there would be no explanation or justification for the companion gift of interpretation of tongues.

It is not difficult to see its effectiveness in arousing interest and causing wonder and amazement as it did on the day of Pentecost. Its value as a sign to onlookers is also clear.

Paul states that the speaker "edifieth himself",[23] even if he does not edify the church as greatly as if he prophesied. There are many who testify to a sense of release, liberty in worship and a new sense of the Lord's nearness and freedom in prayer through the experience. Granted that this may be true, but it is also true that the same release and joy has come to others through the Spirit's working, without speaking in tongues.

Others maintain that it imparts a sense of objective assurance that God is actually doing something in one's life. The direct use of the vocal apparatus by Someone outside oneself gives it the sense of a supernatural sign. This also may be true, but is not the desire for a sign not a mark of spiritual immaturity rather than of maturity? Neither our Lord nor Paul encouraged the seeking of a sign to strengthen faith. Walking by faith is presented as a higher experience than walking by sense and sight.[24] The supreme sign of the supernatural working of God in the life, and one not open to counterfeit, is a transformed life expressed in selfless and loving service to God and man. "By their fruits ye shall know them," was our Lord's test.

Limitations on Value

The fact that the Spirit through Paul hedged the exercise of this gift with certain restraints, indicates that there are limitations on its usefulness where these restraints are not observed.

More than some of the other spiritual gifts, its very unusualness can lead to *preoccupation with oneself and subjective experience*, rather than serving the Church in the highest degree. "He edifieth himself,"[25] indicates that it may be a selfish experience.

It also has *an inherent tendency to divisiveness*, as the whole history of movements majoring in this gift reveals. The evidence of the Spirit's working is unity, not division.[26] This would argue the presence of a good deal that is not the genuine gift of the Spirit, who does not destroy His own work. It is beyond dispute that the exercise of this gift has been a fruitful source of division both in the homelands and on the mission-field. It tends to create a tension between the "haves" and the "have nots", and the impression is given, not always intentionally, that the "have nots" are second-class Christians.

Tongue-speaking is *only one form of prayer,* and is not the most important form, since it by-passes the intellect.[27] Paul stressed the superiority of prayer in which the understanding was fruitful. "I will pray with the spirit, and I will pray with the understanding also," as is the case in "supplications, prayers, intercessions and giving of thanks."[28] In all of these the intellect is consciously engaged.

Because of its spectacular character, it leaves its possessor specially open to *spiritual pride, and a patronizing attitude* towards those who do not have the gift. The possession of other gifts, too, can leave one open to this temptation, but this gift especially so to those who are spiritually immature. It tends to make its possessor a missionary of his own experience.

The disposition *to make this manifestation the sole evidence of the baptism in the Spirit* is a position that lacks Scriptural support. It is possible to speak in tongues and yet not to be filled with the Spirit. If tongues were the sole or even the essential initial evidence of the baptism or filling of the Spirit, then we should seek it above all else. But this is the reverse of the New Testament emphasis. Nowhere is the Christian commanded to seek this gift, At best, tongue-speaking is not to be forbidden.[29]

It is not without significance that the only New Testament church in which the gift is specifically stated to be in exercise, was far from spiritual, but *bore the marks of spiritual immaturity.*[30] Factions, jealousies, immorality, lawsuits, excesses at the Lord's table in the Corinthian church, all tend to show that the possession and exercise of this gift is by no means the hallmark of spirituality and maturity. This does not mean that the gift was not of God, but it does show that it was majored in by Christians many of whom were not notably spiritual. Was it that their unrestrained exercise of the gift had hindered their progress towards maturity?

In his treatment of the subject in Corinthians, Paul was concerned to wean the Corinthians from "an obsessive concentration and delight in the ecstatic and abnormal, and to train them to understand the Spirit's gifts in terms of Christian morals and love". Although permitting tongues, he appears to discourage too great an emphasis on this gift.

Of all the spiritual gifts, this is the one most *open to counterfeit.* Satan delights to imitate and debase all that is good and holy, and pervert it to his own base uses. The psychical and spiritual realms are very closely inter-related, and it is easy to mistake the one for the other.

It may be justifiably asserted that in conventional religion today, the emotional element is unduly suppressed. The opposite tendency, emotional excess, is inherent in the unguarded exercise of this gift. In this connection F. W. Robertson wrote, "The Holy Spirit may mingle with man in three ways—with his body, and then you have what is called a miracle; with his spirit, and then you have that exalted feeling which finds vent in 'tongues'; or with his intellect, and then you have prophecy. In the case of 'tongues' men felt, and could not logically express that feeling. . . . The clear understanding vanished into ecstasy; the utterer, unless he controlled them, was carried away by his feelings."

This state of ecstasy was so pleasurable and so excited the admiration and emulation of others in the Corinthian church, that it became a prime object of pursuit, and drew forth Paul's cautioning words.

It must be borne in mind that tongue-speaking is not a distinctively Christian phenomenon, for it has its parallels in other religions, and cannot be associated solely with the Holy Spirit or the gift at Pentecost. The vocal apparatus can be used by other than God, since the same phenomenon occurs in Buddhism, in Spiritism, in Mormonism, in Hinduism and in Islam.

The Three Occurrences in Acts

It is the widely though not universally held view of those who claim to have this gift, that speaking in tongues is *the essential evidence of the baptism or filling of the Spirit*, and that without it, while a measure of the Spirit's power and presence may be enjoyed, the baptism has not been experienced.

This belief is based on the fact that at Jerusalem on the day of Pentecost, at Caesarea in the house of Cornelius, and at the gathering of John's disciples in Ephesus, the baptism in the Spirit was evidenced by speaking in tongues.[31] A study of these three occurrences reveals, as has been stated earlier, that in each case *a distinctive religious group* was involved, and there was *a significant reason* for the bestowal of this gift.

Jerusalem

The feast of Pentecost had drawn to Jerusalem a great company of *Jews* from surrounding countries. With the great facts of redemption now complete, the stage was set for the descent of the Spirit. In the event, God gave three confirming signs that He had indeed come—the sound as of wind, tongues as of fire and speaking with other tongues. The effect of the latter convinced the crowds that they were in the presence of the supernatural.

It is not stated that the disciples preached the evangel in other tongues, but that they proclaimed "the wonderful works of God". The tongue-speaking caused no conversions, but it did create wonder and amazement and prepared them for Peter's presentation of the evangel. The three thousand conversions resulted not from the tongues, but from Peter's preaching in his own language with which the majority present would be familiar. It would appear, therefore, that the Tongues were evidential rather than evangelistic in purpose. There is no record of an identical repetition on any subsequent occasion.

Caesarea

Here the reason was different. The gift of tongues was rendered necessary by the reluctance of Peter to obey the Lord in taking the gospel to Cornelius, *the Gentile*. His attitude was representative of the church at Jerusalem. In order to convince both Peter and the church that God had bestowed the identical gift of the Spirit on the Gentiles as well as the Jews, God repeated the evidential gift of tongues. It indicated to the bigoted Jews that God recognized no difference between them and the Gentile Christians, who could accept the gospel on the same basis. It gave assurance to hesitant Jewish Christians that they need not hesitate to accept Gentile Christians into their fellowship. It was in effect an extension of Pentecost to Caesarea.

Ephesus

It appears that these Jewish *disciples of John* had heard nothing of the great events that had taken place at Jerusalem, or of the outpouring of the Spirit at Pentecost. Through Paul's explanation of these events and the laying on of hands, they received the like gift, and their experience was linked with that of the Christians at Jerusalem and Caesarea by the same evidential gift of tongues. Pentecost was extended to Ephesus.

Samaria[32]

It is not stated that speaking in tongues accompanied the

131

reception of the Spirit by the Samaritans, but some maintain that this is implied in the statement, "when Simon *saw* that the Spirit was given . . ." This is not a necessary inference, but if it were true, here was another distinct religious group with whom the Jews had no dealings, and there would be the same reason for bestowing the gift of tongues as in the case of the Gentiles.

It is to be noted that in no case did the recipients seek this gift, it was bestowed sovereignly. It was bestowed on entire groups of people, not specially selected or prepared individuals. In each case it came unexpectedly. In each case it was given at one and the same meeting. In each case it was present at the beginning of their Christian experience. There is no specific evidence that any of those who participated ever spoke in tongues again, although of course they may have done so. But the only other record of tongue-speaking is in the church at Corinth.

In these cases the gift of tongues was given as evidence that the identical gift of the Spirit had been bestowed on each group, not as evidence of the baptism or filling of the Spirit. It cannot be maintained on the basis of these passages that tongue-speaking is the sole or indispensable evidence of the baptism or filling of the Spirit. If it were, that would make it the most important spiritual gift, and to be sought above all others. Paul's emphasis, however, is in the opposite direction. Prophecy is everywhere given precedence over tongues.

Significant Omissions

We have noted that beyond the above three occurrences of tongue-speaking in the book of Acts, there is no mention of the gift. It is of interest to note the cases in this book in which speaking in tongues *did not accompany* the filling of the Spirit. There are nine such occurrences, but Pentecost was the only occasion when tongue-speaking resulted.

It is of course unwise to base too much on the argument from silence. Sometimes it proves too much. But it is of significance in this context when so large a superstructure is built on so small a foundation.

Tongue-speaking is not mentioned in the instances when Peter appeared before the Sanhedrin,[33] when the believers were praying together,[34] the appointment of the seven deacons,[35] in the cases of Stephen[36] or Barnabas,[37] Saul at his baptism[38] or of the disciples at Antioch.[39]

There is no mention of the 3,000 converted at Pentecost receiving the gift, and their case would parallel that of Christians today more closely than would that of the disciples in the upper room; nor of the 5,000; nor of the great company of priests. The great majority of those whom Luke reports as coming to the faith are not said to have spoken in tongues.

These facts would indicate that there is little basis for maintaining that speaking in tongues subsequent to the baptism or filling of the Spirit is *normative* in the New Testament.

In this connection, Norman Grubb who does not exclude the possibility of speaking in tongues writes: "There are those, and not a few, who say that there must be a visible evidence of the enduement of the Spirit by the speaking with other tongues as on the day of Pentecost. An examination of the New Testament does not indicate this. Its whole attention is focused on the Person Himself, and not on a particular gift of His. He was the Divine Indweller in the Son of Man, but came on Him as a gentle dove. At Pentecost, in His official entry into the world as the Executive of the Trinity, He came with three mighty accompaniments: tongues of fire, a rushing wind, and the gift of foreign languages. In no known cases in the history of the church has He come again like this, either upon one person as a dove, or upon a company with all these signs at once. That should be proof enough that He comes as He will and in no set way....

"When it comes to the exposition of the life in the Spirit with which all the Epistles are occupied, the sign or gift of tongues is completely ignored, except in the famous chapters of 1 Corinthians in which it is deliberately soft-pedalled. And then it is significant that it is only referred to as a gift which not all had, and never once as the essential sign of receiving the Spirit. If it was of such paramount importance as that the Spirit would surely have led His servant to say so."

Rules Governing Exercise of the Gift

Paul did not question the reality or value of the gift, but he was alive to its dangers. If it be accepted that there may be genuine speaking in tongues, it must be accepted as a corollary that its *genuineness will be attested by conformity to the requirements of Scripture.* From Paul's counsels, the following facts emerge:

The bestowal of all spiritual gifts is the sovereign prerogative of the Holy Spirit, therefore no one gift can be demanded as of right.[40]

There is no Biblical warrant for claiming that all Christians either may or should speak in tongues.[41]

We are urged to desire earnestly the greater gifts, those which are most to the edification of the Church.[42]

The primary object of the bestowal of any gift is the edification of the Church.[43] If any gift does not do this, it is either counterfeit or being abused.

If anyone desires to speak in a tongue in public, he must first ascertain whether one with the gift of interpretation is present.[44]

In the church, speaking in a tongue was to be confined to only two or three, and each in turn. They must speak in succession and not all at once. Failing this, the tongue was to be suppressed, an indication that it could be controlled.[45]

If the exercise of the gift produces confusion rather than order, that is prima facie evidence that it is spurious, for "God is not the author of confusion".[46]

All spiritual gifts that are genuine promote peace and harmony and maintain the unity of the Spirit. Whatever has a divisive and centrifugal tendency is open to suspicion.[47]

A More Excellent Way

Paul's great hymn of love was not placed where it is in the Corinthian epistle by mere chance. Its lofty theme was introduced of set purpose and its objective is clearly stated: "But covet earnestly the higher gifts: and yet I show unto you a more excellent way"—than even spectacular spiritual gifts. It is the way of Christian love. Unless motivated by and exercised in the spirit of pure love, the highest gift is utterly valueless spiritually.

"Make love your aim", pleads Paul, "and earnestly desire spiritual gifts"—but not the one without the other. This is the "more excellent way".

REFERENCES

1. Acts 2:4-7. 2. Luke 24:49. 3. Acts 1:8. 4. Acts 2:4. 5. 1 Cor. 12:30. 6. Acts 2:6. 7. 1 Cor. 14:2. 8. Acts 2:6. 9. 1 Cor. 14:2, 9. 10. Acts 2:6. 11. 1 Cor. 14:23, 28. 12. Acts 11:15. 13. 1 Cor. 14:22. 14. Acts 2:7, 8. 15. 1 Cor. 14:23. 16. Acts 2:1. 17. 1 Cor. 14:33. 18. 1 Cor. 13:8. 19. Heb. 2:3, 4. 20. 1 Cor. 14:39. 21. 1 Cor. 14:18. 22. 1 Cor. 14:5. 23. 1 Cor. 14:4. 24. 2

Cor. 5:7.   25. 1 Cor. 14:4.   26. Eph. 4:3.   27. 1 Cor. 14:14,
15.   28. 2 Tim. 2:1.   29. 1 Cor. 14:39.   30. 1 Cor. 3:1.   31. Acts
2:4, 10:46, 19:6.   32. Acts 8:17.   33. Acts 4:8.   34. Acts 4:31.
35. Acts 6:5.   36. Acts 7:55.   37. Acts 13:9.   38. Acts 9:17.
39. Acts 13:52.   40. 1 Cor. 12:11.   41. 1 Cor. 12:30.   42. 1 Cor.
14:12.   43. 1 Cor. 14:12.   44. 1 Cor. 14:28.   45. 1 Cor. 14:27.
46. 1 Cor. 14:33.   47. Eph. 4:3.

Chapter Seventeen

THE FILLING OF THE SPIRIT

" 'They were all filled with the Holy Spirit'. The words are wonderfully simple, and yet express a truth surpassing understanding. What a vital difference the coming of the Spirit in His fulness to their hearts made to those first disciples. The weak became strong; the timid bold; the carnal, spiritual . . . we may understand the verse to mean that the Holy Spirit took entire possession of them to the full, and imparted to them, to the fullest extent of their capacity, His grace and power."

THOMAS WALKER

"The fulness of the triune God, Father, Son, and Spirit is the Christian's heritage. To make us possessors of this fulness is the work of the Holy Spirit. To do it He must have absolute sway over us through complete control. We must be filled with the Spirit. Fulness imparts to the Christian the power of self-control; animates his heart with new life; brings his spirit, soul and body into correct adjustment; enhances the power of mind, heart and will to fulfil the Divine purpose, and leads to spiritual, moral, mental and physical wholeness."

RUTH PAXSON

"I have heard it argued that all Christians have the Holy Spirit and that therefore it makes no sense to teach some subsequent experience of the Spirit. Have such persons forgotten that our Lord Jesus had the Holy Spirit during all those growing up and maturing years at Nazareth? Have they forgotten that when at the age of thirty He entered upon His public ministry the Holy Spirit came upon Him? The *philosophy* of it is not as important as the *fact* of it—either with Jesus or with you and me."

PAUL S. REES

THE FILLING OF THE SPIRIT

"They were all filled with the Holy Spirit."

Acts 2:4

"Be filled with the Spirit."

Eph. 5:18

The New Testament teaches that God's plan for the Christian is a life of perennial fulness, satisfaction and usefulness in His service. Calvary and Pentecost have made possible the satisfaction of every legitimate aspiration of the regenerate heart, and that this may be realized through the filling of the Spirit is confirmed by a study of the nine instances recorded in the Book of Acts in which the filling was experienced.

It was this experience which effected the amazing transformation in the lives of the disciples. It was the secret of the irresistible power of their preaching. It was the explanation of the amazing signs and results which attended their witness. If this is so, it is vitally important that we understand the doctrine and enjoy the experience of the filling of the Spirit.

The Meaning of the Term

From the contrasting commands, "Be not drunk with wine wherein is excess", and "Be filled with the Spirit", we would be justified in concluding that the person who is filled with the Spirit will be dominated and controlled by the Holy Spirit even as the drunkard is dominated and controlled by his intoxicating wine.

The conception behind the command is not that of an empty vessel passively waiting for something to be poured into it, as water into an empty glass. A better illustration would be that of a house and its owner. The Holy Spirit is to occupy and control the life of the believer in whom He dwells and whom He fills, just as the owner occupies and controls the house in which he lives.

But even this illustration is inadequate, for the Holy Spirit is rather a Person, Who can control another personality. The concept is that of a human personality voluntarily surrendered to the control of the Holy Spirit, Who in turn, imparts powers and qualities that would otherwise be unknown. This is implied in the word "filled", which Thayer defines: "That which wholly takes possession of the mind is said to fill it."

The manner in which the word is elsewhere used supports this definition. "They were all *filled* with fear"[1] when they saw the wonder working power of the Lord, we read. When He was breaking the news of His impending departure to His disciples, He said, "Because I have said these things unto you, sorrow hath *filled* your hearts".[2] What does it mean to have hearts filled with fear, or sorrow? It means that these emotions so grip and control the heart and mind that other things become of only secondary importance. In the heart of the believer who is filled with the Spirit, He reigns supreme over the will, the emotions, the intelligence, but with his full consent and co-operation.

The word carries the idea of being filled to the point of saturation, a fulness that leaves nothing to be desired. We read of Stephen that he was "a man *full* of faith and of the Holy Spirit".[3] Here too it carries the meaning "that which possesses fully or influences fully". So to be full of the Spirit means the habitual experience of having the Holy Spirit in the free and unhindered exercise of all His attributes—knowledge, power, holiness, peace, joy—exercising His sway and dominion in every realm of life.

Perhaps if we eliminate the objectionable features, the imperfect illustration of hypnotism may help in clarifying the significance of the term. A hypnotized person speaks and acts at the behest of another to whom he has yielded control of his will, and says and does things he would not and could not otherwise say or do. In hypnotism, the subject must be passive and allow his mind to go blank, giving himself up to the hypnotist—a dangerous attitude. But there is no passivity in being filled with the Spirit. Every faculty and power of the Spirit-filled man are constantly in full exercise. The Spirit's control is not automatic, but voluntarily conceded and invited. If the surrender of the human personality to the Spirit is withdrawn, as it can be, His control is thereby broken and His power short-circuited.

There arises the metaphysical problem, How can one personality enter another? A. W. Tozer writes in this connection: "The candid reply would be simply that we do not know, but a near approach to an understanding may be made by a simple analogy borrowed from the old devotional writers of several hundred years ago. We place a piece of iron in the fire and blow up the coals. At first we have two distinct substances, iron and fire. When we insert the iron in the fire we achieve the penetration of the fire by the iron. Soon the fire begins to penetrate the iron and we have not only the iron in the fire but the fire in the iron as well. They are two distinct substances, but they have co-mingled and interpenetrated to a point where the two have become one. In some such manner does the Holy Spirit penetrate our spirits. In the whole experience we remain our very selves. ... Now the Holy Spirit penetrates and fills our personalities and we are experientially one with God."

The fulness of the Spirit does not obliterate personality as does hypnotism. In fact it is only when filled with the Spirit that one's true personality is released and fully realized. We will never know the full possibilities of our redeemed personalities until we yield them completely to the Spirit's influence and control.

The indwelling Spirit exercises this control from within, from the centre of the personality. He enlightens the *intellect* so that there is an ever-deepening insight into spiritual truth. He purifies the *emotions* and affections and fixes them on Christ, for His ministry is always Christo-centric. He reinforces the *will*, weakened by sinful indulgence, and imparts power to do the will of God.

The Purpose of the Filling

The purpose is eminently practical. Christ's followers were faced with a superhuman task for which nothing less than supernatural power would avail. The Holy Spirit was the answer to their need.

The context of the command to be filled with the Spirit makes it clear that it is an experience *for every Christian, in everyday life.* In other words it is essential to a normal Christian life. It is not for a spiritual élite or suitable only for extraordinary conditions. It will affect every relationship of life.

The control of the Spirit will have tangible results in domestic relationships.[4] Because the Christian home is the citadel of Christianity, Paul, guided by the Spirit shows how Spirit-filled believers will deport themselves in the exacting relationships of home and family life. He addresses wives, husbands and children in turn, indicating the role each should play in the ideal home, if filled with the Spirit.

Then, too, business relationships[5] will feel the impact of the Spirit's control of lives. The relationships between masters and servants will be sweetened. Servants will be faithful and masters considerate.

The experience is *for ordinary Christians in ordinary Christian service*. When a crisis of social service arose in the early Church, the solution was to find Spirit-filled men[6] to administer the finances and carry out the social service. The fulness of the Spirit is not primarily for working miracles or ecstatic experience. It is for hidden service in which God is glorified and the Church built up.

But it is also *for specially-called Christians for special work*. Peter, imprisoned with John, is called on to defend the activities of the infant Church before the High Priest. Much hangs on the wisdom and cogency of his answer. In the filling of the Spirit he received power and wisdom to answer his adversaries.[7] He was similarly equipped and aided by the Spirit in his clash with Elymas the sorcerer.[8]

In spite of their innate cowardice, this divine enduement enabled the apostles to preach the Word with boldness.[9] Their fire-impregnated words went home with irresistible power.[10] While the stones were raining on his battered body, Stephen, full of the Holy Spirit, forgot his own suffering in the joy of the supporting presence of Christ, and in the intensity of his intercession for his persecutors.[11]

> "With one accord, until the mighty gift
> Of Pentecostal power was outpoured;
> Then forth as witnesses possessed of God,
> To preach the resurrection of the Lord."

The Manifestation of the Filling

Since no two people are identical either physically or temperamentally, it is self-evident that the results of the filling will vary with the individual. Who would expect the same reactions in the cautious Scot and the mercurial Irishman? The Holy Spirit does not override the laws of the mind. We should leave the manifestation to the sovereign Spirit, rather than seek to emulate the experience of another. The manifestation He gives will best equip us for the part we have to play in the service of God and the Church.

But apart from special manifestations, there are certain results which may always be expected. The experience will always be *Christ-centred, not Spirit-centred*. "He shall glorify me,"[12] said our Lord. In the life which He controls, *the Spirit will make*

141

Christ vividly real. Was this not one of the distinguishing features of the experience of the early Christians? It seemed as though He was at their very elbow as they witnessed. He became to them the home of their thoughts and the home of their affections.

Again, *He will form Christ in the believer.*[13] The life of Christ defies imitation, but the method of the Spirit is not imitation but reproduction. The measure of His success is the measure of the freedom we give Him to remove that which mars Christ's image in us, and to impart the virtues of Christ which are lacking. One filled with the Spirit will inevitably grow more and more like his Lord.

Further, *He will impart His own power.* "Ye shall receive power after the Holy Spirit is come upon you."[14] He who is filled with the Spirit will be spiritually powerful. Eloquence and rhetoric may arrest the mind, but they cannot move the spirit Godward. It requires the power of the Spirit.

There may not always be the *consciousness* of power, even when it is present.

In the early days of this century a well known evangelist went to a practitioner for special electrical treatment. He was asked to sit in a chair while the doctor read a newspaper. After waiting sometime, the evangelist asked that the treatment might begin.

"You are being treated now", was the answer.

"But I can feel nothing at all", he replied. Then the physician took a board with several lamps and placed it against his chest. Instantly they glowed with light.

"There is enough power passing through your body to run the street car, but you do not feel it because you are insulated," he was told.

We may have the mighty power of God passing through us, and yet be unconscious of it because there is no special call for its use. But let the need arise and the power will be manifested, for it is there.

Conditions for the Filling

There are no "Three easy steps" to the experience of the Spirit's filling. It does not come automatically, or to unprepared hearts. From the tenor of Scripture it would appear that there will first be *aspiration.* "The soul of the sluggard desireth and hath nothing."[15] It is they who "hunger and thirst"[16] who are satisfied. "I will pour water on him who is thirsty,"[17] is the promise. "If any man thirst..."[18] We are unlikely to know this experience if we do not aspire to know it.

Dr. Jonathan Goforth experienced a growing dissatisfaction with his work. Restless and discontented, he was led to a more intensive study of the Scriptures. "Every passage that had any bearing upon the price of, or the road to the accession of power became life and breath to me...", he wrote. "If Finney is right then I am going to find out what those laws of the Spirit are, and obey them no matter what the cost." Such an attitude always commands the blessing of God, as it did with him.

It needs to be said that our aspiration should have the glory of God in view. Even the desire to be used by God can be an unhallowed ambition.

True aspiration will lead to *acknowledgment* of the absence of this divine blessing. When we repent of the sin of disobedience to God's command to be filled with the Spirit, He can then lead us on to the further experience.

There must of necessity be an *abandonment* of sin consciously tolerated in the life. "If I regard iniquity in my heart the Lord will not hear me." Doubtful things should be surrendered and wrong things renounced.

The descent of the Spirit was dependent on the glorification of Christ. The filling of the Spirit, too, is dependent on the enthronement of Christ in the life of the Christian, and this will involve *abdication* of the throne by the usurper Self. Where self is on the throne of the heart, God would be condoning this usurpation were He to fill it with His Spirit.

When we have honestly complied with God's requirements in so far as we know them, we can confidently count on God's faithfulness to His Word, and *appropriate* the promised fulness.

It is just at this point that many come short of the blessing. The naked Word of God seems too unstable a foundation for such a revolutionary experience. Reflecting his own experience, Dr. F. B. Meyer wrote: "Reckoning that God has kept His Word with you, dare to believe it, though you may not be conscious of any emotion, and you will find when you come to work, or to suffer, or to meet temptation, that there will be in you the consciousness of a power which you have never known before, and which will indicate the filling of the Spirit."

Maintaining the Experience

It is one thing to become Spirit-filled, but another to remain Spirit-filled.

Since the fulness of the Spirit is possible on the grounds of our union with Christ, it will continue as we *keep abiding* in Christ.[19] The initial crisal experience will not suffice of itself. It must be followed by abiding in Christ.

Since God has given the Holy Spirit to them that obey Him,[20] we are to *keep obeying* the will of God as it is revealed to us.

Since we remain filled with the Spirit so long as we are filled with the Word, we are to *keep feeding* on it. This is borne out by the fact that the results which follow being "filled with the Spirit", are exactly the same as follow letting "The word of Christ dwell in you richly".[21]

Since it is the Spirit's delight to honour and glorify Christ, if we are to please Him, we too will *keep occupied with Christ*. The fillling is not an end in itself. Christ is the end.

> *"Father, by this blessed filling,*
> *Dwell Thyself in us we pray!*
> *We are waiting, Thou art willing!*
> *Fill us with Thyself today."*

REFERENCES

1. Luke 5:26.   2. John 16:6.   3. Acts 6:5.   4. Eph. 5:22, 6:4.
5. Eph. 6:5-9.   6. Acts 6:3.   7. Acts 4:8.   8. Acts 13:9-11.
9. Acts 4:31.   10. Acts 6:10.   11. Acts 7:60.   12. John 6:14.
13. Gal. 4:19.   14. Acts 1:8.   15. Prov. 13:4.   16. Matt. 5:6.
17. Isa. 44:3.   18. John 7:37.   19. John 15:4.   20. Acts 5:32.
21. cf. Eph. 5:18 ff. with Col. 3:16 ff.

Chapter Eighteen

THE FRUIT OF THE SPIRIT

"We come to 'the fruit of the Spirit'. It is *fruit*. You will notice the word is in the singular—not *fruits*, as we generally say, but *fruit*; which will emphasise the thought that if there be nine different virtues in this category, it is not that nine different persons are to manifest these virtues, but it is that each person is to have the nine. It is not that one has joy, another peace; but every man has love and joy and peace and all the rest of them."

W. Y. FULLERTON

"These fruits, though they are the direct results of the indwelling Spirit and will never be produced without His presence, are none the less truly dependent upon our manner of receiving that Spirit and on our faithfulness and diligence in the use of His gifts. It is, alas! sadly true, and matter of tragically common experience that instead of 'trees of righteousness, the planting of the Lord' heavy with ruddy clusters, there are but dwarfed and scrubby bushes which have scarcely life enough to keep up a little show of green leaves and 'bring no fruit to perfection.' Would that so-called Christian people would more earnestly and searchingly ask themselves why it is that, with such possibilities offered to them their actual attainments should be so small."

ALEXANDER MACLAREN

THE FRUIT OF THE SPIRIT

*"Now the works of the flesh are these ... But the fruit
of the Spirit is love, joy, peace, longsuffering, gentleness,
goodness, faith, meekness, temperance."*

Gal. 5:19, 22, 23

"I have chosen and ordained you that ye should go and *bring
forth fruit*,"[1] said our Lord in His parting message to His
disciples. Fruitbearing had been the theme of His preceding
conversation, and He emphasized the importance of what
He had been saying by giving this as one of the purposes
behind His choice of them. Peter never forgot the lesson, and
after enumerating eight Christian graces in his letter, added
these words: "If these things be in you and abound, they make
you that ye shall be neither barren nor unfruitful..."[2]

This attractive cluster of fruit presents a perfect portraiture
of Christ, in whose life it appeared in a luxuriance and profusion
never seen in this world, before or since. It was Schliermacher
who said that the fruits of the Spirit are the virtues of Christ. It
delineates, too, the ideal Christian life, for Christian character
is essentially the fruit of the indwelling Spirit, who will not be
content until there appear in the life the virtues of Christ.

The beauty and attractiveness of the fruit is only enhanced
by the inky blackness of the background against which it is set.
Paul has just completed a catalogue of the works of the flesh.
Seventeen manifestations are given, but this by no means ex-
hausts the list, for he adds, "and such like". What a foul brood
they are! Four types of sin are named. (1) Sins of misdirected
physical desire—in the realm of *sex*. (2) Sins of misdirected
faith—in the realm of *religion*. (3) Violations of brotherly love—
in the realm of *society*. (4) sins of excess—in the realm of
drink.

The works of the flesh outnumber the fruit of the Spirit,
bearing out the words of A. R. Faussett, "It is a proof of our
fallen state, how much richer every vocabulary is in words for sin
than in those for graces". Archbishop R. C. Trench drew attention to the fact the Tasmanian native had scores of words
for "infanticide", but not a single word for "home" or "love". It

is sobering to remind ourselves that our own hearts are capable of harbouring any one in this sorry list of sins.

It will be noted that Paul contrasts the "works (plural) of the flesh" with the "fruit (singular) of the Spirit". At first sight it would seem that in this sentence the rules of grammar are violated: "The fruit of the Spirit *is* love, joy, peace, etc."? Paul has not, however, employed the wrong number, for the works of the flesh are separate acts performed by man, while the ninefold fruit of the Spirit is the issue of the one life within.

The use of the singular number emphasizes the unity and coherence of life in the Spirit, in contrast with the disorder and instability of the life dominated by the flesh. The fruit is not conceived of as so many separated graces, but as all springing from the same root, and constituting an organic whole which is the creation of the Holy Spirit. The life which finds its unifying centre in Christ produces a harvest of love which has varied expressions. It is entirely beyond the power of man to produce or even imitate this fruit. It is inwrought and outworked by the Holy Spirit Himself, for the fruit is what we are rather than what we *do*.

Many interesting analyses of this outcome of the Spirit's activity have been attempted. Archbishop H. C. Lees developed the thought of the Spirit's fruit under the similitude of a garden in which nine flowers flourish: the honeysuckle of love, the rose of joy, the lily of peace, the snowdrop of longsuffering, the mignonette of kindliness, the daisy of goodness, the forget-me-not of faithfulness, the violet of meekness and the wallflower of self-control.

Dr. C. J. Rolls characterized the fruit as the eight elements of love. Joy is love's cheerfulness. Peace is love's confidence. Long-suffering is love's composure. Kindliness is love's considerateness. Goodness is love's character. Faithfulness is love's constancy. Meekness is love's comeliness. Self-control is love's conquest.

The nine elements are divisible into three triads. The first describes the ideal life *in its relation to God*, the second *in its relation to our fellows*, and the third *in relation to ourselves*. Or to express it differently, the fruit is manifested in the realm of experience, in the realm of conduct and in the realm of character.

The Triad of Experience—Love, Joy, Peace.

Because these three graces were present in perfection in the

147

life of our Lord, they can and should be the experience of those who are united to Him by faith. There is no limit to the measure in which the Spirit-filled believer may enjoy them. He can experience "the love of Christ which passeth knowledge,"[3] "joy unspeakable and full of glory,"[4] "peace which passeth all understanding".[5] God bestows His best blessings in the superlative.

Love is given first place in the list, since all the other manifestations of the fruit are but various forms of love. It is the foundation and moving principle of all the others. It is not mere human love, but the manifestation of "the love of God which is shed abroad in our hearts by the Holy Spirit".[6] It is the Spirit's pleasure to produce in the Christian's heart a deepening sense of God's love, and the disposition to love Him in return.

But He goes further. He imparts a more than human love that embraces the unlovely as well as the lovable. Indeed it includes even enemies. Such a fruit is no native of earth.

The Spirit produces *Joy*. Not the mere merriment or happiness that comes from having no troubles. It is something much deeper than that, a divine grace. Happiness and unhappiness do not exist together, but joy and sorrow can and do.[7] The heart filled with the love of God rejoices with "joy in the Holy Spirit".[8] It can be experienced in the midst of much affliction. The Spirit imparted this joy to the Thessalonian Christians in the midst of tribulation,[9] paradoxical though that may seem. Christ was "a Man of sorrows and acquainted with grief", yet He was "anointed with the oil of gladness above his fellows".[10] Before His death He bequeathed His joy to His disciples, and as Executor of Christ's will,[11] the Spirit delights to carry out its provisions.

Peace is the inner tranquillity and harmony enjoyed by the believer who is living in conformity to the will of God. This, too, was part of Christ's legacy to His disciples. "Peace I leave with you."[12] It is a Spirit-imparted serenity which guards the heart against invading cares,[13] and has its source in a quiet confidence in God. Brother Lawrence used to talk of sheltering in the bosom of God, and was even unselfishly troubled to think that the flowers of peace which grew so easily and naturally in his heart, seemed to be missed by others. The secret was, of course, that he offered no obstacle to the working of the Holy Spirit in his life. This peace is not the automatic outcome of favourable circumstances, but the supernatural product of the Spirit, whatever the circumstances may be.

> *"Thy sevenfold grace bestow upon us freely:*
> *Love, deep and full, to God and all mankind;*

148

Joy in the Lord, 'mid every earthly sorrow;
Peace, calm and sweet, that guardeth heart and mind."

The Triad of Conduct.—Longsuffering, gentleness, goodness.

This second triad of social virtues, is the exhibition of the fruit of the Spirit in our relations with our fellow-men.

Longsuffering is rendered in several contemporary translations as "patience", but there is something to be said in favour of the older word, since the reference is less to patience under adverse circumstances than to suffering the follies and cruelties of one's fellow man. It is patience towards *people*, those who aggravate or persecute one.

It certainly means forbearance, and slowness to avenge wrongs suffered, a refusal to retaliate. Said a tyrant to a Christian whom he had in his power financially, "What can Christ do for you now?" "He can help me to forgive you," replied the Christian.

This fruit is frequently mentioned as an attribute of God, Who is "longsuffering and abundant in goodness and truth".[14] It is well for us that this is God's character. Love's greatest triumph is achieved, not in what she does, but in what she refrains from doing. Our Lord set us a shining example in this: "Who when He was reviled, reviled not again; when He suffered, He threatened not."[15]

Gentleness, according to J. B. Lightfoot, is a kindly disposition towards one's neighbours, or *kindliness*. Like longsuffering, it expresses God's attitude towards people. He saves them in order "that in the ages to come He might show the exceeding riches of His grace in His kindness towards us through Jesus Christ."[16] Our kindliness of disposition is to be the reflection of "the kindness and love of God our Saviour".[17] This is not a weak, sentimental quality, for gentleness is power in reserve. It is strong and helpful. "The gentleness of Christ,"[18] reproduced in the believer by the Holy Spirit, makes him "gentle unto all men".[19]

Goodness has been called by Dr. A. Z. Conrad, "an abandoned waif—neglected, abused, misunderstood. Of royal blood, yet snubbed, sneered at and avoided. Highest and holiest in the category of virtues, yet disowned and undesired. Call a young man 'good' and he will resent the accusation and proceed to demonstrate that he has been falsely accused, by engaging in some wild adventure."

But goodness is much different from the common conception, for it is active beneficence. It is always practical. It was an outstanding characteristic of our Lord Who as an outcome of

His anointing by the Holy Spirit, "went about doing good".[20] Like his Master the Spirit-controlled believer will manifest "the fruit of the Spirit in all goodness".[21] Goodness is more than a kindly disposition; it is a kindly action which must find expression, as in the case of Dorcas who was "full of good works".[22]

> "Make us longsuffering, 'mid earth's provocations;
> Gentleness give us, when enduring wrong;
> Goodness impart that we e'en foes may succour;
> Faithfulness grant, to change our toil to song."

The Triad of Character—faithfulness, meekness, self-control.

Conduct is the outshining of character. What I do is determined by what I am. The fruit of the Spirit, therefore, to be complete, must be expressed in holy and wholesome character. The final three of the nine manifestations of the fruit, grow on the same parent stem. Faithfulness comes of a spirit that is meek because self-controlled.

First comes *Faith* or rather *Faithfulness*—fidelity, trustworthiness. It is not faith in the sense of belief in God that is primarily in view here, but the faithful discharge of entrusted duties. Dr. Gill, however, contends that faith in Christ must not be excluded from the meaning of the Greek word, though fidelity may also be present. A faithful man is one who is full of faith, full of confidence in God, and therefore dependable.

It was for this Christ-like element in his character that God commended Moses. "Moses was very faithful in all his house as a servant."[23] Of Christ it was said that He was "faithful to him that appointed him".[24] The servant is not greater than his Lord.

Pentecost resulted in an astounding transformation in the character of the disciples in this respect. Only a few days previously they had all proved faithless to their Master and had left Him to suffer and die alone, forsaken by God and man. But when filled with the Spirit, they proved faithful under the most fearful persecution; Some were "faithful unto death", and received the "well done!" reserved by the Master for the "good and faithful servant".[25]

Meekness is the most unpopular and least desired of Christian virtues, probably because its meaning is the least understood. It is essentially a Christian grace which was despised by the ancient world.

It must first be understood that meekness does not imply a

weak, vacillating or supine nature. It is not the "greasy servility" of the Uriah Heep variety. That it is the reverse of weakness is clear from the fact that our Lord drew attention to it as one of the noble elements of His own character which we should emulate. It was said of the mighty Moses that he "was very meek, above all the men which were upon the face of the earth".[26] But he could not be charged with weakness.

Aristotle taught that a virtue was the mean between two extremes. Meekness has been said to be the mean between too much and too little anger. It is anger on a leash, for it is to be remembered that anger is one of the greatest of moral dynamics. Our Lord demonstrated this in His cleansing of the temple. The word is also used of an animal that has been domesticated and is responsive to its master's command. In Greek ethics it was used of a man who does not press for the last penny of his rights.

Here, then, are some sidelights on this little-coveted quality which our Lord said was one of the sources of blessedness.[27] The Christian in whose heart the Spirit is producing this fruit will be reasonable yet not weak, yielding yet not spineless, responsive to His Lord's will, and willing to renounce his rights in the interests of his fellow-men.

Meekness is an exotic, it is not native to the human heart. It is the antithesis of pride and arrogance. Man says, "The *aggressive* shall inherit the earth. The world is yours if you can get it." Jesus says, "The *meek* shall inherit the earth. The world is yours if you renounce it."

Never was the dynamic and conquering power of meekness more clearly exhibited than in Him Who said, "Learn of me, for I am meek and lowly in heart".[28] In measure as we purpose to learn of Him, and afford the Spirit full liberty to reproduce His likeness in us, we shall partake of this desirable grace, and will "walk worthy of the vocation wherewith we are called, with all lowliness and meekness".[29]

> "O may that mind in us be formed
> Which shone so bright in Thee;
> A humble, meek and lowly mind,
> From pride and envy free."

The last of the ninefold cluster is *Temperance*, or better *Self-control*. The word means literally "holding in with a firm hand". Grimm defines it as the mastering all one's appetites and passions, especially (though not only) the sensual ones. It is a quality which perhaps more than any other, differentiates man from the lower animals.

Paul illustrates the meaning of self-control from the Greek games. "Every man who striveth for the mastery is self-controlled in all things."[30] Unwholesome food, alcoholic liquor, soft indulgences were abjured as unfitting for a contestant in the games. The same is no less true of the Christian athlete who is competing in the heavenly race. He will "keep his body under, and bring it into subjection", lest he be disqualified.[31]

But we shall entirely miss the point if we fail to remember that this self-control is not the result of the energy of the flesh, but is the fruit of the Spirit. It is not the control of self by self. Paul contrasts the self-control of the Spirit-filled man with the excesses of the reveller.[32]

For the Christian, "self control" connotes the subjugation of the self-life in its myriad forms and manifestations, the bringing of the whole nature under the control of the Spirit. It is the outcome not of stern self-repression, but of the powerful working of the Spirit within.

Paul portrays the situation graphically: "I say unto you, order your lives by the Spirit's guidance, and there will be no fear of your gratifying the cravings of your sensual nature. For the sensual nature passionately resists the Spirit, as does the Spirit the sensual nature; these two are mutually antagonistic, so that your good impulses are thwarted by the one, your evil by the other. But if you definitely surrender yourself to the Spirit's guidance, you are then not under the law, but on a higher plane."[33]

We may count on the Spirit within to produce all nine manifestations of this fruit, by reproducing Christ in us—or as Paul puts it, by forming Christ, in whose life each of these qualities were seen to perfection, in our own lives.[34]

> "*Meekness bestow, with humble self-abasement,*
> *And self-control, through Thy controlling might:*
> *And as we list to every call of duty*
> *May we do all as in Thy searching sight.'*

REFERENCES

1. John 15:16. 2. 2 Pet. 1:8. 3. Eph. 3:19. 4. 1 Pet. 1:8. 5. Phil. 4:7. 6. Rom. 5:5. 7. 2 Cor. 6:10. 8. Rom. 4:17. 9. 1 Thess. 1:6. 10. Heb. 1:9. 11. John. 15:11. 12. John 14:27. 13. Phil. 4:7.

14. Exod. 34:6. 15. 1 Pet. 2:23. 16. Eph. 2:17. 17. Tit. 3:4.
18. 2 Cor. 10:1. 19. 2 Tim. 2:24. 20. Acts 10:38. 21. Eph. 5:9.
22. Acts 9:36. 23. Heb. 3:5. 24. Heb. 3:2. 25. Matt. 25:21.
26. Num. 12:3. 27. Matt. 5:5. 28. Matt. 11:29. 29. Eph. 4:2.
30. 1 Cor. 9:25. 31. 1 Cor. 9:27. 32. Eph. 5:18. 33. Gal.
5:16–18. (Way). 34. Gal. 4:19.